Healing
SECRETS

Healing SECRETS

Self-Medicating Our Most Important Relationships

Jade Chris Mangus

CFI
Springville, Utah

This is not an official publication of The Church of Jesus Christ of Latter-day Saints. The opinions and views expressed herein belong solely to the author and do not necessarily represent the opinions or views of Cedar Fort, Inc. Permission for the use of sources, graphics, and photos is also solely the responsibility of the author.

ISBN 13:978-1-59955-318-4

Published by CFI, an imprint of Cedar Fort, Inc., 2373 W. 700 S., Springville, UT 84663
Distributed by Cedar Fort, Inc., www.cedarfort.com

LIBRARY OF CONGRESS CATALOGING-IN-PUBLICATION DATA

Mangus, Jade Chris.
  Healing secrets : self-medicating our most important relationships / Jade
Chris Mangus.
     p. cm.
  ISBN 978-1-59955-318-4
  1. Interpersonal relations--Religious aspects--Church of Jesus Christ of
Latter-day Saints. 2. Psychotherapy--Religious aspects--Church of Jesus
Christ of Latter-day Saints. I. Title.
  HM1106.M36 2010
  158.2--dc22
                                    2009046622

Cover design by Megan Whittier
Cover design © 2010 by Lyle Mortimer
Edited and typeset by Melissa J. Caldwell

Printed in the United States of America

10 9 8 7 6 5 4 3 2 1

Printed on acid-free paper

To my wife, Jeralyne,
and my kids, Sadie and Seth

CONTENTS

INTRODUCTION

WHEN I WAS IN GRADUATE SCHOOL, I ran across a quote that changed my entire perception: Nietzsche described personal purpose so eloquently when he said, "He who has a *why* to live can bare with almost any *how*." I realized then that I could accomplish anything I wanted to if I simply had a purpose behind it. However, as I began my training as a therapist, I realized that many people may have a *why* and a *how*, but still cannot accomplish a goal, grow, or change. I became aware of the many psychological blocks that stunt growth within people; even if they had a reason and instructions, it still seemed as though they didn't have ability. I thought to myself, "That is strange . . . my client is ready and willing to change. He has a reason and he has acquired the skills, so what is the problem? Why doesn't he change?" One of the answers was revealed to me as I began to notice my interaction with my clients—Eureka! It is the relationship that heals, and these clients cannot do relationships. In essence, people don't grow unless they are in a securely attached relationship.

I have discovered that half the problems that bring people to therapy result from a failure to grow up and stop alienating themselves. This seems to be a sickness that has increased from year to year in our society as a whole. And as people begin to focus on themselves and not on their relationships and community around them, they begin to isolate themselves. This then in turn increases negative relationships, which prompts a person to hide himself from the world even more. Our society as a whole is becoming more self-oriented and focused on the four preoccupations that are destructive to seek: power, gain, lust, and popularity. Dysfunctional relationships are the symptom of society, but true loving and charity, found through sacrifice and compassion, are the remedy.

I wish to explore the ways to overcome this toxic cycle of alienation: to learn to grow and heal by gaining meaning in life and remembering that the true purpose of life is to serve others.

The things that will destroy us:

POLITICS WITHOUT PRINCIPLE;
PLEASURE WITHOUT CONSCIENCE;
WEALTH WITHOUT WORK;
KNOWLEDGE WITHOUT CHARACTER;
BUSINESS WITHOUT MORALITY;
SCIENCE WITHOUT HUMANITY;
WORSHIP WITHOUT SACRIFICE.

Mahatma Gandhi

SECTION ONE

LOVE
&
ALIENATION

Discussion 1

So-Called Love

Darkness cannot drive out darkness; only light can do that. Hate cannot drive out hate; only love can do that. Hate multiplies hate, violence multiplies violence, and toughness multiplies toughness, in a descending spiral of destruction. The chain reaction of evil must be broken, or we shall be plunged into the dark abyss of annihilation.
—Dr. Martin Luther King Jr.

TODAY IN OUR GLOBALIZED WORLD, THERE are many goods for trade: the latest hand-held scheduler that can also be a handheld video game and phone; the new car with built-in televisions installed overhead to turn the children into willing drones; and yes, even love! I am not decrying industry; video games, televisions, and the Internet are wonderful tools, if used in moderation. But when industry and products act as addictions and distractions—especially when they distract from the spiritual—the outcome will always be negative. I have personally witnessed the destructive force of something as simple as a video game acting as a means to destroy a marriage. Through her gaming, a married woman became involved with another man.

The Internet today is a wonderful instrument used by many to exchange goods. People will post their profiles online and discuss all of the wonderful little tidbits about themselves. Oftentimes, people online are genuinely interested in finding "love," and authentic love *can* be found through this media; nevertheless, in the vast majority of instances, these sites promulgate the opposite of love: isolation.

In many ways, the concept of achieving love through the Internet, phone, or other designs of our technological world gives someone a feeling of hope for the future of our community, for people are still trying to find love. Besides searching for love on the Internet, people revel in love through watching romantic movies and listening to erotic music. Definitely, the desire for love is there, and with desire comes hope. However, if we do not know where to look for love or how to achieve love, hope dwindles to extinction.

One problem with the modern concept of love is the idea that love means being loved instead of loving others. Indeed, *loving* as defined by Western society is a sort of loving "internally-externally," or more properly termed, "narcissism." One can often hear, "You need to fall into love." Accidents do happen. But is love an accident? Does love "just happen"? Of course many people attempt to help the accident occur, and they do this by making themselves attractive. The construct of adorning onself with a plume of beautiful feathers can take many forms: the masculine traits of achievements, power, and affluence, or the feminine traits of aesthetics or adornment. As with the lone surfer of the waves of personal home pages, what wares can she or he bring to the table to attract or be loved?

If our Western world has a misconception about love, then what is that misconception? It is the "accident" of falling in love. You know how the story goes: Once there was a young man walking down the street, who walks past a corner market. In a rush, a young woman in the market hurries outside and proceeds to crash into the young man. At first they don't look at one another. He begins to help the young woman pick up her groceries, which have fallen to the ground. He says, "I'm sorry I didn't—" Then their eyes meet, their hearts beat, and they crash into love!

This scenario may have happened to someone once before and there may have been a "sudden spark," but is this sudden spark "love," or is it an urge of a physical nature and less of a spiritual one?

Now to continue on with the story: The two begin to date and the sensations of passion are found in each moment that they are together. Their two hearts beat as one, and they know that they were made for each other. Their emotional bond leads to a physical one as they consummate their loving union. They decide to get married, because they are "soul mates." They live happily ever after.

However, you also know the all-too-common sequel to this story: After some years of love and marriage, and two and a half children, the couple begins to contemplate. "I have played my cards right, I am successful in my business and hobbies, I have a good family with a good spouse. So why am I lonely, dissatisfied, bored, and uneasy?" The union eventually ends, as 50 percent of current unions do, and the couple files for divorce. What went wrong with this couple? And since divorce is an epidemic in our society, what is going wrong in our society?

Love Destroying Shame

As a foundation for our continual discussions, I wish to introduce the concept of *dysfunctional shame*, contrasted from *functional shame*. In functional shame, a person realizes that it is okay to make mistakes, that we are not perfect, and that if we fall down, we can get back up. Dysfunctional shame, on the other hand, can destroy a person. And dysfunctional shame always stems from alienation and avoidance. Please consider the graph on page 8.

The cycle is thus: as a person alienates himself from the society around him, the response to that alienation from others is avoidance, which engenders a feeling of abandonment within the person who then alienated himself (a self-fulfilling prophecy).

When you disconnect, the following things happen:

1. People run from you
2. You feel abandoned
3. You feel unlovable
4. You act out
5. You pay for acting out

The second stage of the graph, *abandonment*, can also stem from other sources than alienation. For instance, abuse of any kind increases feelings of abandonment. When a child is physically, emotionally, or sexually abused, that child negatively detaches from the world around her. Feelings of abandonment are feelings of isolation from human contact. Feelings of abandonment are also feelings of betrayal. These feelings inevitably lead to apathy—an emotion quintessentially tied to alienation.

Feelings of abandonment can also stem from a perception of loss. For instance, a child's father could have been cold and aloof. This father could have also been authoritarian in parenting style—a type of "drill sergeant" parent. This child may then perceive a loss of a father who "could have, should have, and ought to have been" (distortions of thought) a warm and affirming father. This loss has a natural outcome of emotions tied to abandonment.

This abandonment then creates a false self-identity or an identity

THE CYCLE OF DYSFUNCTIONAL SHAME

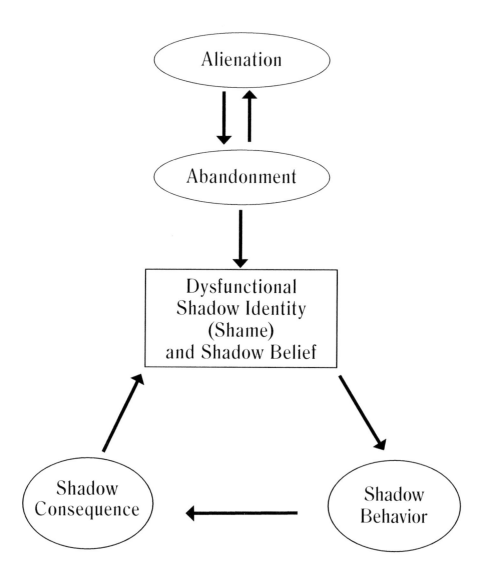

fraught with distorted perceptions of "who am I?" This is the *dysfunctional shadow identity.* And when a person finds himself living through this identity, the perception of self is one of destruction. Persons with this identity may say to themselves, "I am worthless all of the time," or "I am wicked and am not worth God's time . . . or for that matter anybody else's time." This dysfunctional shadow identity is directed by unhealthy shame, which tears a person down and inhibits emotional growth.

When someone has developed a dysfunctional shadow identity, he then begins to live through this identity. His thoughts and beliefs become skewed and distorted, and he develops a "shadow belief." For example, a person might begin to believe that nothing ever works out for him or that no one will ever love him. These shadow beliefs are wrought with non-meaningful pain and suffering, which a person inevitably feels compelled to rid of.

The strong negative emotions that result from the shadow belief lead to the compulsive and addictive actions of the *shadow behaviors.* Drug addiction, gambling, overeating, overspending, and other deviant addictions and compulsions come with a high price to pay. When the *shadow consequences* occur, resulting from negative choices, the results of these choices feed back into the dysfunctional shadow identity, which lead to a self-fulfilling prophecy: "See, I knew it, I am worthless, and the proof of this is the fact that I am in jail for a DUI."

Functional shame is closely related to our authentic selves. To perpetuate and reinforce the authentic self, an individual must accomplish a few necessary steps. The following acronym REAL SELF lists a few steps needed in progressing toward an authentic self:

> **R**ely on God
> **E**xpress emotion
> **A**ccept sources of shame
> **L**et go
>
> **S**elf-disclose
> **E**voke accountability
> **Lo**ve yourself
> **F**orgive yourself and others

RELY ON GOD

Relying on God is essential to heal from any malady. As will be highlighted in discussion 11, I believe that in any relationship, spirituality must be highlighted for the relationship to grow. And concerning therapy, a person's spiritual side must be addressed before ending that therapeutic relationship. The spiritual core values are what lead to lasting change. They make all of the behavioral skills and introspection processed in the therapy sessions take on meaning and purpose, which will lead to lasting change. *If there is no why, how long will the how last?*

Of course, spiritual change is something personal and can only truly be obtained by communion with deity through prayer or meditation.

EXPRESS EMOTION

Expressing emotion is also necessary in obtaining a healing experience. If you have ever attended therapy, you realize that more often than not the therapist asks, "How are you feeling" or "Would you identify your mood for me?" Why are these specialists so interested in moods? For one thing, an exploration of emotions is neglected in our society; to not experience your mood is a good way to develop lasting mental abnormalities. To identify your mood is the gateway to managing your mood. And managing your mood leads to emotional maturity and mental wellness.

I have discovered in my practice of psychotherapy that most mental disorders have a root cause in abnormal emotion maintenance. I have seen both children and adults make great gains in therapy by simply and frequently identifying their moods. Many times, I have seen participants connect psychological patterns and unlock unresolved trauma or grief by opening up emotionally. Your emotions are the gateway to unconscious mysteries that may have been plaguing you for years. Alice Miller, a developmental psychologist and author who is noted for her work on child abuse, essentially stated that exposure to a trauma doesn't cause a mental illness, but rather the inability to express emotion about the trauma causes the dysfunction.

One technique that I have used to help clients obtain their emotional goals is to have them keep a journal and write down the moods that they experience every day. Another technique I have used (especially with children) is to use a "cheat sheet," which has a list of moods. I will have the person take the cheat sheet home and identify a mood off the list several

times during the day. This activity will increase exposure to emotion iden-
tification, which is the first step in emotional management.

ACCEPT SOURCES OF SHAME

For many people this is one of the most difficult steps, because many
individuals' sources of shame can be found within their family. Mother
and Father are our greatest models and sources of love and self-identity.
However, when a family becomes dysfunctional, these models of attachment can wreak havoc on our sensitive and developing sense of self. But
it must be understood, if our parents were toxic, there was probably a
good chance that their parents were toxic as well. If, as a child, a person
was beaten for bad behavior, what other model did he have of parenting
than that of an abusive example received from his parents? This toxic-
ity becomes multigenerational, but, of course, this is not an excuse. Our
agency dictates that we must choose to break the cycle, or we will be as
responsible as those who abused us. And to break this cycle, we must
accept our past, focus on today, and influence our future.

If you have been seriously abused, you must get therapy if you are to
ever get to the point of acceptance. And acceptance will lead to breaking
the cycle.

Note: Acceptance and approval are different. Acceptance is tied to forgiveness, understanding, and letting go. Approval is related to condoning.

LET GO

Tied to relying on God is letting go. A common Alcoholics Anonymous phrase is "Let go and let God." Surrendering control is what letting
go is all about. One of the most powerful aspects of any twelve-step group
is the recitation of the Serenity Prayer.

> God grant me the Serenity
> To Accept the things I cannot change
> The Courage to change the things I can
> *And the Wisdom to Know the difference.*[1]

Acceptance of things that are out of our control is often one of the
most difficult things to perceive when we attempt to overcome love-
destroying shame. Another key element that relates these concepts of letting go and accepting is the idea of *detaching.*

Detachment doesn't mean that we don't care. It does mean that we are involved but within healthy self-boundaries. With detachment comes serenity, because we reach a state of being in which we can observe the environment around us, but we don't have to control the environment. *We are in the world but not of the world.*

For example, I had a client who would obsess and worry about seemingly everything, but specifically her teenage son. The son was severely addicted to narcotics. When her son turned eighteen, he went to jail on drug charges, and my client was immediately present to bail him out. She attempted to do everything for him, and she wondered why her son would continue to get into trouble. She would rescue, and he would rebel. Finally, my client came to the realization that her son needed to be "his own man." Again he was sent to jail, but she did not bail him out. She told him that she loved him but that he needed to take responsibility for himself—she detached but was still involved and loving toward him. To her surprise, her crippling depression, anxiety, and anger issues slowly faded, and she then no longer needed to see me for therapy.

Self-Disclosure

To overcome the shadow identity and dysfunctional shame, a person must self-disclose to others. Self-disclosure is essential—it leads to a corrective emotional experience, which is a healing process of overcoming the damage done from earlier dysfunctional relationships. This is the power behind recovery and therapy groups. When we come out of hiding and reveal pain to a supportive group of people, we overcome our shadow identities and come closer and nearer to our authentic selves. This leads to developing healthy relationships, which also adds to the corrective emotional experience.

Evoke Accountability

The majority of people I see in therapy are there because they do not want to make a decision—they want me (their therapist) to make a decision for them. When I think of almost every mental or relational problem I have helped people with, there inevitably is a responsibility issue at the core of the matter. This is what the defense mechanisms of projections, displacement, splitting (triangulation), and others are defending against—personal accountability!

(Notice how many of these defense mechanisms deal with responsibility avoidance at an unconscious, preconscious, and conscious level).[2]

Level 1 Defense Mechanisms

This strategy of defense is almost always severely pathological. The mechanisms under Level 1 permit a person to rearrange his external reality and eliminate the need to cope in a more effective manner. Oftentimes, people who primarily use these strategies appear to others as crazy or insane. However, these are found mainly in childhood. Here are few examples:

Denial: Refusal to accept external reality because it is too threatening. I once had a client who was extremely "stuck" in his addiction, even to the point where he denied that he had cirrhosis of the liver because of his drinking. No amount of evidence that the medical doctors gave him convinced him that he had this disorder, because it meant that he would have to give up drinking—one of his only ways to cope with his anxiety.

Distortion: A severely skewed view of external reality. For example, a person may distort his reality by believing that he is a no good loser, who won't amount to anything. But the subtle message is, "Don't ask me to do anything, because I am incapable."

Delusional Projection: Gross delusions about external reality, usually of a persecutory nature, or in other words, "Everyone is out to get me! And they really do mean me harm." Delusional Projection is simply paranoia.

Level 2 Defense Mechanisms

These defenses are present in adulthood but more often seen in adolescence. These mechanisms help a person minimize distress and anxiety found in negative or uncomfortable relationships to others. Again, keep in mind, defense mechanisms are often healthy, but when they become dysfunctional, dangerous, or debilitating, things go awry. Others often perceive people who use Level 2 defense mechanisms excessively as socially undesirable or immature people who are seriously depressed or have a personality disorder. However, in adolescence, all of these defenses are reasonably normal. These include:

Fantasy: A type of isolation. People often use fantasy to escape reality. A pornography addiction is an example of someone using this defense.

Projection: Projection is a primitive form of paranoia. A person reduces his anxiety by allowing the expression of the undesirable impulse or desire without becoming consciously aware of it, attributing one's own unacknowledged, unacceptable, or unwanted thoughts and emotions to another. Examples might be: "I don't have a problem, you have the problem!" severe prejudice, severe jealousy, and injustice collecting.

Hypochondriasis or somatization: This is the transformation of negative feelings toward others or oneself into illness or anxiety. Oftentimes, this defense has to be ruled out by emergency room staff because a person may have severe physical pain with no source but emotional distress.

Passive Aggression: These are the "backstabbers" or people who have hidden agendas. They will say something passive to your face, but their behavior is aggressive. One of the strongest examples of this was a woman I worked with who was fired from her job because she knifed her boss's tires. She saw herself as a "people pleaser" and a "yes women." Her boss would often ask of her things she did not desire to do, but instead of being assertive and getting her needs met, she silently built up resentment until she knifed the tires. And she was also stealing office supplies, because she felt she deserved them and that they were her compensation."

Level 3 Defense Mechanisms

These mechanisms are also know as neurotic defense mechanisms. They have a short term advantage in coping with anxiety; however, they can severely disrupt interpersonal relationships. These include:

Displacement: This mechanism shifts sexual or aggressive impulses to a more acceptable or less threatening target. For instance, I had a client who had been molested as a child. He often was unconsciously sexually aroused by children because of being molested himself. However, he was severely addicted to pornography and masturbation to the point that no therapeutic strategy seemed to help him. It wasn't until he became aware of his sexual desires toward children, and worked through them, that his addictions stopped.

Dissociation: A person may separate himself from an emotion that would normally accompany a situation or thought to protect himself from anxiety. A client of mine stated that she was distressed at her father's funeral because she felt no emotion. In fact, she stated that she felt a little humorous, if anything.

Intellectualization or Isolation of Affect: People may be excessively intellectual in anxiety-provoking situations. They separate emotions from ideas; they think about wishes in formal, emotionally bland terms and do not act on them. When asked, "How do you feel?" they will respond, "I don't know." They really do not know!

Reaction Formation: Converting unconscious wishes or impulses that are perceived as dangerous into their opposites, or taking the opposite belief because the true belief causes anxiety. For example: Your family loves corn, and they love it so much that they would punish you for not liking corn, but you hate it. Eventually, you believe that you like corn.

Repression: Process of pulling thoughts into the unconscious and preventing painful or dangerous thoughts from entering consciousness; seemingly unexplainable naiveté, memory lapse, or lack of awareness of one's own situation and condition; the emotion is conscious, but the idea behind it is absent.

Level 4 Defense Mechanisms

These are common among those considered by many to be emotionally healthy. Though they have their roots in immaturity, they are seen as being mature ways to defend.

They can enable a person to self-master and enhance in progressing toward some goal. I will only give two examples of these defenses, because they are tangential to our discussion on responsibility avoidance. These include:

Sublimation: The process of taking negative emotions or instincts and transforming them into positive actions or emotions. A surgeon may have been a child who liked to abuse animals. He transferred this aggressive impulse into an action that benefits society.

Suppression: The conscious process of pushing thoughts into the preconscious. Another name for this would be "disengaging." Essential suppression is an action taken by someone who is under stress and delays paying attention to that stress in order to cope with the present situation. For example, a couple I was helping would often argue relentlessly in the morning, go to work, and then come home and continue the argument. They were able to go to work and function as though no conflict had taken place at home.

Defense mechanisms protect us from being consciously aware of a thought or feeling that we cannot tolerate. The defense allows the unconscious thought or feeling to be expressed indirectly in a disguised form. When these defenses become dysfunctional, dangerous, deviant, or distressing, a person needs to seek treatment; however, it is essential to know that many of these defenses operate within all of us. These defenses are not inherently negative; some may be quite positive, like sublimation. Many of these defenses can contribute to responsibility avoidance.

For example, I once worked with an individual who was in extreme denial about his heroin addiction. He had convinced himself that it was natural and even healthy for him. He felt that everyone was out to get him, and as long as he could maintain his job and his relationships, there was no reason to change. In a therapy group for substance abuse, many of the group members tried to "break him." They would challenge and confront him until they were literally blue in the face. However, none of their efforts worked. One day he presented the group with a depressed affect that was unlike his usual bravado. He stated, "My girlfriend left me, and I think I am going to get fired, all because of my drug use." His defenses were down, and the group could get some real work done. He seemed ready, willing, and somewhat able to grow out of this dysfunction—or so we thought.

As the group gave him suggestions and praised him on "seeing through the pink haze," he began to become a bit stoic. He then began to follow the group's lead by asking for advice, which they in turn were eager to give. Over the next week, he practiced the behaviors that the group told him to do, began a twelve-step program as they had advised, and attempted to be as honest as he could with others, also as the group had advised.

During the next group meeting, he was absent, and he never returned. "What happened?" group members asked. "He was doing so well." On a private phone call I had with him some weeks later, he told me that the twelve-step group was full of "self-righteous do-gooders," the people he'd attempted to be honest with had rejected him, and all the advice the group had given him had "blown up in his face." He has made the group accountable for his failed attempts at sobriety.

How do we evoke accountability within ourselves when we may be in a state of defensiveness? It has much to do with our relationships with others and how they respond to us. Good feedback from those who care does not include advice; it will only perpetuate responsibility avoidance. Good listening is key to evoking accountability.

Thomas Gordon, psychologist and specialist in the field of addiction therapy, described some roadblocks to listening:

- Asking questions
- Agreeing, approving, or praising
- Advising, suggesting, providing solutions
- Arguing, persuading with logic, lecturing
- Analyzing or interpreting
- Assuring, sympathizing, or consoling
- Ordering, directing, or commanding
- Warning, cautioning, or threatening
- Moralizing, telling others what they "should" do
- Disagreeing, judging, criticizing, or blaming
- Shaming, ridiculing, or labeling
- Withdrawing, distracting, humoring, or changing the subject

Why are they roadblocks? Gordon explains that they get in the speaker's way. In order to keep moving, the speaker has to go around them. They have the effect of "blocking, stopping, diverting, or changing direction." They insert the listener's "stuff" and communicate the "one-up role": Listen to *me*! I'm the expert. And they put-down (subtly, or not-so-subtly).[3]

Certainly, it is a difficult, if not an impossible, job to evoke accountability in others, and often it is difficult to evoke accountability in ourselves. The first step is to realize that we do not want to investigate many aspects of our lives. The second step is to become aware of the fact that we are responsible for those aspects; we are even responsible for things outside of ourselves. In a strange way, it can be liberating to know that we are responsible for everything in our environment—we are not to blame, but we are responsible. It is also key to remember that freedom is found in two simple actions: repenting and forgiving (we will discuss more about this in the next section).

LOVE YOURSELF

This is a powerful principle. Loving yourself will be described throughout this book as one of the quintessential achievements to overcome most mental dysfunctions. The first step is to become familiar with positive affirmations. There is power in intently looking into your eyes in a mirror and saying, "I love you. You mean a lot to me," and so on. We often do just the opposite. If a person attempts to give himself positive affirmations continuously for two weeks, that person will notice a drastic change in the way he perceives himself and his environment.

When a lawyer asked Jesus, "Master, which is the great commandment in the law?" he answered, "Thou shalt love the Lord thy God with all thy heart, and with all thy soul, and with all thy mind. This is the first and great commandment. And the second is like unto it, Thou shalt love thy neighbor as thyself" (Matthew 22:36–39). Notice that Jesus said you are to love your neighbor as yourself. God wants you to love yourself just as much as he wants you to love others. Dr. Clark Swain stated, "If you truly love yourself, you will remember that you are a physical, mental, and spiritual being. Loving yourself as God wants you to means that you use wisdom in protecting your life and conserving your health."[4]

Loving yourself also means being grateful for yourself and your abilities and being grateful to God. Research has shown that an attitude of gratitude can significantly increase a lasting sense of well-being. In an experimental comparison, those who kept gratitude journals on a weekly basis exercised more regularly, reported fewer physical problems, felt better about their lives as a whole, and were more optimistic about the upcoming week, compared to those who recorded hassles or neutral life events.[5]

A related benefit of the attitude of gratitude was observed in the realm of personal goal attainment: Participants who kept gratitude lists were more likely to have made progress toward important personal goals (academic, interpersonal, and health-based) over a two-month period compared to subjects in the other experimental conditions. Moreover, daily gratitude interventions (self-guided exercises) with young adults resulted in higher reported levels of alertness, enthusiasm, determination, attentiveness, and energy compared to a focus on hassles or downward social comparisons (ways in which participants thought about how they were better off than others). There was no difference in the levels of unpleasant emotions reported in the three groups. It was also found by Drs. Robert A. Emmons and Michael E. McCullough that in a sample of adults with neuromuscular disease, a twenty-one-day gratitude intervention resulted in greater amounts of high-energy positive moods, a greater sense of feeling connected to others, more optimistic ratings of the subjects' lives, and better sleep duration and sleep quality, relative to a control group.[6]

FORGIVENESS OF SELF AND OTHERS

This section is a little longer than the former because this concept is essential to healing. All people need to learn two principles to overcome the shadow identity: repentance and forgiveness. Repenting is essential because this action leads to an understanding that we make mistakes, that we are not perfect, and that we are "okay" when we do something wrong, say sorry, and make restitution. Asking God for forgiveness is liberating and evokes healthy shame and guilt, which John Bradshaw suggests will safeguard the soul because we can conceptualize that we have boundaries and are good people who perform badly at times.[7] Again, it is "okay"; we must not be so hard on ourselves.

The danger of the shadow identity is that an individual can become dichotomous in thought, action, and belief. On one extreme a person may need to be perfect, achieving very well in everything. This person is also compelled to show little to no emotions, because he believes this is a weakness. These people "have to" and "have no choice" in their need to achieve. On the other side of the shadow identity spectrum is an individual who sees himself as a "no-good sinner" and not worthy of redemption. Both sides of the spectrum are toxic and can lead to personal destruction.

The Greek word for the English term *repentance* denotes a change of mind, or in effect, a fresh view about God (Bible Dictionary, "Repentance," 760). This idea is at odds with the notions of punishment and pain, with which many people associate the term *repentance*.

Forgiveness of ourselves is important, and forgiveness of others is essential for our healing. Anyone who has ever been victimized—and that includes survivors of crime, accidents, childhood abuse, political imprisonment, warfare, and so on—must decide whether or not to forgive those who made the violation, even if that person is not repentant. There can be no way around this choice: either you decide to forgive the person who hurt you, or you hold on to bitterness and anger until it consumes you. Holding on to bitterness and anger can perpetuate further bitterness and anger.

One example I witnessed was an individual who had been molested by a grandfather, who had passed away without ever acknowledging his wrongdoing. The survivor's anger and desire for revenge became an obsession. She focused so much on the crime that she completely missed her opportunity to learn about real love, forgiveness, and letting go. Instead, she seemed to believe that hatred would satisfy her thirst for vengeance and would somehow bring healing. As a result, this individual repeated over and over, "I'll never forgive."

One of my favorite examples of a character who didn't forgive is Darth Vader. He was so preoccupied with those who trespassed against him that his hatred and revenge literally turned him into a machine. What a powerful archetype Darth Vader is of vengeance.

Forgiving can be a problem for some to conceptualize because it can be an obscure concept. We as a society have been bombarded by the ideas of "getting even" and "mercy is for the weak." And many times, the concept of forgiveness gets confused with the concept of reconciliation, which is related to forgiveness. *Reconciliation* and *restitution* are even more closely related than *forgiveness* and *reconciliation*, although all three terms are orbital. *Restitution* "denotes a return of something once present, but which has been taken away or lost" (Bible Dictionary, "Restitution," 761). *Reconciliation* comes from the Latin words *re-*, meaning "again," and *conciliare*, which means "to bring together."

Again, the difficulty surrounding forgiveness is an understanding of the difference between reconciliation and forgiveness. And in many instances persons who have wronged another do not "own up" to their mistakes, especially when pride is involved. Thus, restitution does not happen and reconciliation doesn't take place. And when reconciliation is not present, then what is the victim to do? Most victims don't realize that forgiveness is a choice on their part, no matter what the victimizer does or does not do.

Furthermore, if the victimizer seeks reconciliation, that action and healing can only occur if the victim is willing and able to forgive. Forgiveness is always the victim's, or the survivor's, decision. In addition, reconciliation is impossible unless the victim is willing and able to forgive *and* the victimizer apologizes or restores that which has been taken or was lost. Now I have used the words "willing and able" because there is something problematic concerning forgiveness—you cannot fully forgive until you allow yourself to feel the pain you were caused. And in our Western society, it seems that everyone attempts to avoid pain, or any other emotion for that matter.

This is why forgiveness can be tricky. If we don't experience that pain, something much more toxic will take its place—anger and revenge. This occurs because a person who does not express pain unconsciously builds resentment. This resentment, as it builds, needs to find an outlet. This outlet may be a physical one, such as hypertension or headaches. However, usually the outlet is a more psychological one, such as depression or anger (turned outward or inward toward one's self).

I once worked with a gentleman who, after twenty years of work, was fired because of office politics. He came in to see me because of an addiction to pain pills. He was a very sophisticated individual and saw himself as an enlightened and intellectual individual. In groups, this man would make wonderful insights about other group members. He revealed one day that he felt he was addicted to anger. Anger began to fill the void that drugs had occupied. He began to say in group therapy, "Those jerks took away my job . . . I did nothing wrong. They were intimidated by me and because of their power issues they fired me." Of course, his former employer made no restitution, so therefore he could "never forgive them," although at the time of his firing he had said to his wife, "Oh, well, it's not that big of a deal. I'm just going to forget about it." He had prematurely forgiven his employer, which led to resentment and an addiction to pain pills.

Psychologically, the concept of "forgetting" is called "repression." And when something is repressed, it hangs around under the surface, needing expression somehow, physically or emotionally. When pain is repressed, it drags down all the emotions associated with that pain, thus making forgiveness impossible, because on some level you are just "keeping score." *Forgiveness is not the same thing as forgetting.* To forgive is simply to stop wishing for revenge or to stop wanting to see the other person suffer in some way. But forgiveness is not blind. Because trust has been violated, you cannot just forget what happened or else the same thing might happen again.

The steps and the cycle to our authentic self are found on page 22.

As the graph reveals, this cycle is the antithesis to the shadow cycle. And as oil and water repel each other, so do the shadow and the light. As one increases in light, one's shadow's self diminishes.

A negative self-fulfilling prophecy occurs in the dysfunctional shadow identity cycle: negative beliefs lead to negative shadow behaviors, and negative shadow behaviors lead to negative shadow consequences that continuously feed the dysfunctional shadow identity. In the authentic self

STEPS AND CYCLE TO AUTHENTIC SELF

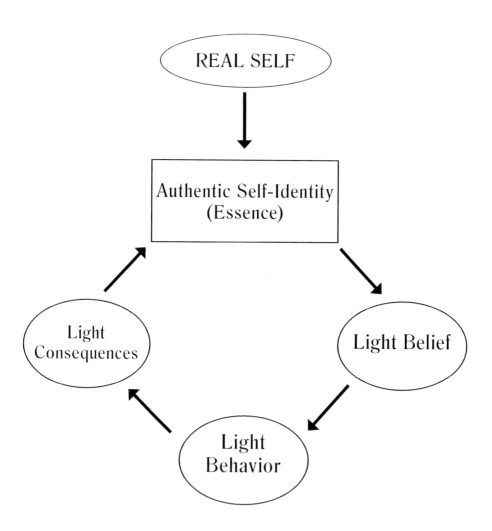

cycle, light beliefs, such as "I am a good person" lead to light behaviors, such as serving others, which lead to light consequences that create a positive self-fulfilling prophecy, which thus feeds the authentic self.

Notes

1. Alcoholics Anonymous World Services, *Alcoholics Anonymous "The Big Book"* 3rd ed. 1976. From web based "blue book" (under "AA traditions"). See www.alcoholicsanonymous.com.

2. See F. Garrett, "Addiction and Its Mechanisms of Defense," http://www.bma-wellness.com/papers/Addiction_Defenses.html, and C. E. Tucker-Ladd, "Stress, Trauma, Anxiety, Fears, and Psychosomatic Disorders," *Psychological Self-Help,* http://www.psychologicalselfhelp.org.

3. Thomas Gordon, "Blocks to Listening," as stated in William R. Miller and Stephen Rollnick, *Motivational Interviewing: Preparing People for Change,* 2nd ed. (New York: Guilford Press, 2002), 49, 68.

4. Clark Swain, "Q&A: Questions and Answers," *New Era,* Mar. 1979, 37–38.

5. R. A. Emmons and M. E. McCullough, "Counting Blessings Versus Burdens: Experimental Studies of Gratitude and Subjective Well-being in Daily Life," *Journal of Personality and Social Psychology,* 84 (2003), 377–89.

6. Ibid.

7. John Bradshaw, *Healing the Shame that Binds You* (Deerfield Beach, FL: Health Communications, 1988), 3–23.

Discussion 2

ALIENATION

Is it that we as a society have merely eroticized love too much?
—Anonymous

WHEN A YOUNG COUPLE BEGINS TO question the validity of their marriage, a profound fear and sinking feeling arises: "We are not in love anymore!" And in the scenario mentioned earlier, the young man and woman realize that, on some level during this time, they have been alienating.

If we look at the problem of alienation, we can consider three major components: the psychological, the social, and the spiritual. A person's psychological need for a sense of security and identity often conflicts with realistic needs and potential. To act in accordance with realistic needs is often risky and threatens the narcissistic side of a person—those wares that were used to initially attract the love object. Essentially, an individual sells out his own growth for security. He holds to the narcissism out of fear and seeks to escape from the realization of what has been done.

Our Western world supports the alienation process through seduction. The world provides its citizens with an abundance of oversimplified values and easy answers, which negate the very essence of life's purpose: to actively serve others. Those who are in the thralls of selling their wares to attract others will easily adopt these values. Both the media and science uphold these values as well as the "self-help" gurus who promise quick answers to life's pressing issues. "Twenty seconds to happiness" cannot, and probably should not, be achieved, even if it were possible. Many people believe that concepts such as happiness are a destination that can be arrived at. The fact is that happiness is a process, not a destination, and must be actively nurtured throughout an individual's life.

Again, concerning the psychological and social components: alienation can somewhat be remedied through these spheres, but essentially the spiritual component must be present to overcome the problems of alienation. If a person focuses on the spiritual, then many of these other components will fall into line.

Indeed, when it has come to mental wellness, for some years now psychology has espoused a concept of focusing on the cognitions, affect, and behaviors of the organism to overcome mental "disease." And in fact, until recently, to discuss the spiritual side of human nature was taboo in psychotherapy, thus leaving out an essential part of mental well-being. This might explain the high recidivism rates in many areas of therapy, especially in the areas of addiction. Of course, it is necessary to focus on thoughts, behaviors, and emotions in therapy; however, all will be unraveled if the spiritual is not addressed along with the rest.

Moreover, if an individual only focuses on the emotions, behaviors, and cognitions of life—as many therapists would have a participant in therapy do—this will essentially lead to the very isolation, or alienation, that was a causal factor in the person's dysfunction. Indeed, most of the modern therapy techniques used with the public are generally focusing on a person's internal view, which in turn further entrenches the person into a deeper self-aggrandizement.

As was discussed earlier, self-loving is not a negative attribute; an individual needs to love himself in order to love others. However, when this loving turns into inward obsession, it will be destructive for the self. A focus on the spiritual can and will eventually lead to a grand understanding of what mental health truly is.

Edwin E. Gantt in "Hedonism, Suffering, and Redemption" stated: "[The] individual who settles for the evanescent pleasures of mortal flesh is a fool who will fail in the end to secure that which is the most truly gratifying of all pleasures: eternal communion with God."[1]

In psychotherapy, communion with the spiritual has been minimized to a type of "opiate of the masses" and that the "pleasure principle" rules supreme. This results in questions like, "What will lead a person to the greatest amount of pleasure?" and "Does pain and suffering have no place in the experience of life?"

Not only does psychotherapy lead to this notion of ruling out pain to achieve pleasure (which we will soon see leads to greater alienation), but medicine espouses a reduction of pain and even a reduction of the human experience as a whole.

A disclaimer: medicine and psychiatry do have an important role in human function. Many psychiatric disorders must be attended to by the art of psychiatry. However, to "treat" every mental "illness" with psychotropic meds is both unnecessary and dangerous for society as a whole. The medical model is one of reducing the individual down to a label or minimizing a person to a diagnosis (hence, the term *shrinks*, when applied to therapists who shrink people to their diagnoses). This is a convenient system for those "treating" the person who manifests a symptom; however, are people their symptoms? Is a person with schizophrenia a schizophrenic or a person who suffers from schizophrenia? This is a very important distinction. (Indeed, even many of the "symptoms" of schizophrenia could be reduced if there were more focus placed on eradicating alienation.)

There is a need for medications to help with dysfunctions, but these medications need to be used as an aid in overcoming isolation, not as a crutch to substitute a person's active pursuit of his goals. In many instances, medications only exacerbate alienation because they mask the essential issues that a patient needs to focus on. Indeed, many times prescribed medications are used in much the same way as illicit drugs—as an avoidant coping strategy.

At the spiritual level, we realize that answers and solutions to the major issues in human existence are not easily forthcoming. The problem is that an individual may not be primarily alienated from his self. Nor is he primarily alienated from other people, for he may have achieved a significant level of compromise with others. A person may have even freed himself from social restraints that seek to change who the person essentially is. The real problem is that the person who has become a self-fulfilling being has opened an experience of existence that can cause a great deal of anxiety—that of dread (I will discuss the issue of dread later, but at this point I just want to emphasize that this element will lead to further alienation). At this junction of existence, a person will stop growing and will utilize an avoidant coping strategy, such as prescribed medication, illicit drugs, watching television, overeating, getting lost surfing the web, and so forth. If we truly look at our society as a whole, we can find many more "mental disorders" than we would have first considered, and they are all influenced either directly or indirectly by alienation.

NOTE

1. Edwin E. Gantt, "Hedonism, Suffering, and Redemption," *Turning Freud Upside Down: Gospel Perspectives on Pyschotherapy's Fundamental Problems*, eds. Aaron P. Jackson and Lane Fischer with Doris R. Dant (Provo, UT: Brigham Young University Press, 2005), 57.

SELF-LOVE

This know also, that in the last days perilous times shall come. For men shall be lovers of their own selves, covetous, boasters, proud, blasphemers, disobedient to parents, unthankful, unholy, without natural affection, trucebreakers, false accusers, incontinent, fierce, despisers of those that are good, traitors, heady, high-minded, lovers of pleasures more than lovers of God; having a form of godliness, but denying the power thereof . . .
—2 Timothy 3:1–5

WHAT CAN WE PURCHASE? AS STATED previously, we can acquire almost anything if we have the purchasing power to back it up. And indeed, every facet of our lives is now driven by the agenda of corporations. In this world of acquisition through wealth, many plain and precious substances of the human condition are being reduced to objects for purchase. And as stated before, even the concept of love is being traded on the open markets of the world.

This reduction of love to an object of trade has led to objectification of the human being. This objectification has in turn led to a narcissistic society, evidenced by personal self-interest ruling out the common good. We can see this all around us in our society, perpetuated by the media and science. The ideas of psychology have turned us toward introspection to make us oblivious to the world around us.

And as stated previously, love has been turned inward as well—loving others has been refocused to *being* loved by others or being a personal admirer of oneself. So why is it that those who are "into" themselves end up being the very people who have the highest level of self-loathing? If this is love, why is there so much hatred and aggression toward the self that accompanies this self-interest?

By now, there have been many allusions to the definition of narcissism, or as psychoanalytic writing discusses, a love turned inward. In

1 Nephi 22:23, Nephi gives insight into four things people should never look for, things that lead to a consuming narcissism, or a destruction of the spirit. First, you should never aspire for gain. Second, you should avoid a desire to obtain power. Third, avoid attempting to be popular. And fourth, avoid lust, for it can destroy a person.

Many can recollect from grade school their study of the Greeks and the story of Narcissus, from whom "narcissist" was derived. Narcissus was an object of obsession for the Greek goddess and nymph Echo. This obsession was not mutual for Narcissus, which led to the death of the nymph because of grief and sorrow; the same malady befell many who admired Narcissus. The beauty this youth possessed was an attraction for both men and women, but the attraction was not returned, and Narcissus was unmoved by their passion. On one occasion, as Narcissus was passing some calm water, he stopped to drink and saw his reflection in the water for the first time. Finally, the young Narcissus was obsessed, but it was with his own reflection. In an attempt to possess his self-image, he jumped into the water and drowned.

When one considers the tale of Narcissus, one can see many powerful parallels to our current situation. First, there are people who are obsessed with others; as with Echo, this obsession is not love, and oftentimes the object of an individual's obsession does not share the obsession, leading to further despair and codependence. Obsession cannot be true love, for obsession is synonymous with possession or selfishness. The person who is possessed with this attitude cannot love nor truly be loved, for theirs is an attitude of self-interest and ultimately exploitation of others. Possession and obsession will lead to jealousy and envy, two symptoms of despair, as well as depression or neurosis.

Obsession belongs to Narcissus as well, for he ultimately became self-involved and obsessed with himself. His world became a world turned inward, as reality exists for many in our society.

As hinted at above, Narcissistic individuals do not love themselves too much; they actually love too little. They are caught up in a sort of ego idolatry; however, it is only a façade. Previously, I discussed the distinction between love turned inward (narcissism) and self-love. Sigmund Freud stated that "the selfish person is narcissistic and has withdrawn his love from others and turned it toward his own person."[1] Perhaps Freud's usage of narcissism as love turned inward should be reworded as object interest turned inward as opposed to object interest turned outward, because a quintessential narcissistic person cannot love.

Now with this new term "object interest" we can better understand the obsession of Echo the nymph. This was not love, but object interest turned outward. Another form of object interest turned outward is very seductive and is in reality only a form of narcissism. That is of those who are "seen of men" doing "good works." This is also a malady of our current society, for many corporations and people donate large amounts of money to charity organizations or do charity work for either political clout, tax write-offs, or other reasons. On the surface, these charitable contributions can look like acts of true charity (certainly there are times when it is true charity); however, if observed closely, it becomes apparent that these acts are done so the general public notices them. As Jesus said: "They have their reward" (Matthew 6:2), and the popularity of these acts cancels out the potential of true love and charity that could have accompanied them.

Dr. Clark Swain stated, "Conceit comes from comparing yourself to others and concluding that you are better than they are. Comparing yourself to others can also result in either feelings of inferiority or superiority."[2] Psychologist Maxwell Maltz says an inferiority complex and a superiority complex are merely opposite sides of the same coin. And the coin is counterfeit, for no one is either inferior or superior to anyone else.[3] A person is just different from others. Accept yourself as the unique person that you are without comparing yourself to others. Doing so will help you love yourself properly without conceit.

Let us consider some of the probable causes of narcissism, or unhealthy object interest turned inward or outward.

Psychoanalytic writing determines that within the narcissist there may be arrested development during childhood. More specifically, at some point in the early life of a child, probably around the ages of two, three, or four, the child became emotionally "fixated" at this stage of life. This fixation continued through adolescence and into adulthood, stunting this person's emotional growth. Psychoanalysts claim that a fixation is the result of cold and rejecting parents or the parents' failure to properly empathize with and validate the child's sense of uniqueness or vigor. As a result, disturbances occurring in self-perception, or more specifically, the child's "grandiose" self and "reality-based" self, which normally would develop beyond the aforementioned ages, remains mostly grandiose, and that person is then endowed with a sense of desirability and power.

Now to keep from becoming too dichotomous in thought, one must realize that in some circumstances the psychoanalyst has an appropriate theory. This theory has held true in many cases concerning matters of children of abuse; children whose parents have died; children who have been adopted; or children caught in the middle of a divorce. In certain cases this can be a causal factor in this idea of unhealthy self-involvement, but can this theory explain the predominance of so much narcissism in our society?

Another thought on the subject would have one conceive narcissism this way: unhealthy self-interest develops as a result of people being treated too positively rather than too negatively in early life. This line of thought sees those who exhibit narcissism as having acquired a grandiose, or superior, sense of self from parents who perpetuated this view, reinforcing these attitudes by doting and spoiling the individual. In defense of this line of thought, many firstborn or only children who are viewed by parents as having special gifts or high levels of intelligence have been found to have higher levels of narcissism.[4] Again, this idea of narcissism can be true for many cases, but can it explain the high rates of narcissism in our society?

Finally, one last theory of narcissism looks at the social and even cultural aspect of narcissism. This idea is formulated through an analysis of family values, social mores, and folkways, which produce a generation of self-centered and materialistic youth. And indeed, the Western world emphasizes and perpetuates these ideas of individualism, competitiveness, and self-expression.

As a brief side note: at times, narcissism becomes more than just a dysfunctional part of the self—it becomes dangerous. Welcome to the realm of the ultimate rebel—the sociopath—whose only concern is for himself at the expense of others. This individual lives on impulse, has no concept of the future, and is detached from reality. If our society becomes a sociopathic society, only chaos will rule.

Thus far, we have considered narcissism, or the more esoteric term of negative object interest turned inward. Cited in many writings on the subject, the term *narcissism* has been mistakenly defined as "self-love." This idea has been deliberately readjusted to define narcissism as unhealthy self-interest or self-obsession, because self-love is indeed a concept that belongs on the opposite end of the spectrum from narcissism.

Self-love can be difficult to understand, if an understanding of the spiritual side of the human condition has not been achieved. We start on a journey to self-love by serving others. "If you love yourself, you love everyone else as you do yourself. As long as you love another person less than you love yourself, you will not really succeed in loving yourself, but if you love all alike, including yourself, you will love them as one person and that person is both God and man. Thus he is a great and righteous person who, loving himself, loves others equally."[5]

This quote has many components similar to Christ's admonition when he said, "Thou shalt love the Lord thy God with all thy heart, and with all thy soul, and with all thy mind. This is the first and great commandment. And the second is like unto it, Thou shalt love thy neighbor as thyself" (Matthew 22:37–39).

Christ and the unknown author were not speaking of narcissism, for the narcissist would not love his neighbor; indeed, as stated before, narcissists hate themselves.

As suggested earlier, we must learn to love ourselves and then love all others before a true concept of love can come to fruition. But how does an individual learn to love himself and all others? It is not just through knowledge where this answer lies, but through doing—for through knowledge and action comes wisdom, and through wisdom and continual service comes love. There are no easy answers in life, and love is not easy—it takes effort. As highlighted earlier, there are no quick fixes, and the way to the transitory effects of love is an uphill battle, but true knowledge and wisdom comes in no other form, as will be seen.

Notes

1. Sigmund Freud, *Psychopathy of Everyday Life (1938)* in *The Basic Writings of Sigmund Freud,* trans. and ed. A. A. Brill (New York: Modern Library, 1995), 440.

2. Swain, "Q&A: Questions and Answers," 37–38.

3. Maxwell Maltz as quoted by Swain, "Q&A: Questions and Answers," 37–38.

4. J. M. Curtis and D. R. Cowell, "Relation of Birth Order and Scores on Measures of Pathological Narcissm," *Psychological Reports* 72, no. 1 (1993): 311–15.

5. Unknown author

Discussion 4

THE INDIVIDUAL AND THE COMMUNITY

All that we are is the result of what we have thought. The mind is everything. What we think, we become.
—Maharishi Mahesh Yogi

MANY INDIVIDUALS FIND THEMSELVES IN ONE of five character states or "camps." Reasons for an allegiance to these camps may have to do with genetics, environment, or psychic makeup. However, all of these allegiances have to do with choice.

Each of us creates our own reality, or in other words, our own paradigm. And to change these realities can be difficult but often necessary.

It must be emphasized that through the following analysis, individuals can only have traits that are comparable with these camps, for everyone is his or her own diagnostic category. Thus, it must be realized that the following camps are for understanding, not for labeling.

The camps are flexible, and by choice an individual can navigate in and out of each criterion. And indeed, as you will see, at times we can have our proverbial foot in two or three camps within a short period of time.

THE BIASED

This is the camp that all narcissists inhabit; for the biased, the world revolves around them and their own needs are of salient importance to themselves. However, this camp is too broad to be inhabited by only the narcissists, for this camp has been described in psychological theories in terms of "defenses." The biased is in defense toward

35

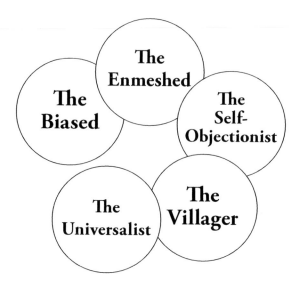

more community-oriented ideas of reality. Developmentally, this camp would be attributed to a dependent person, for the biased is truly in a state of reliance on other people for their support. And in contrast with the narcissist, a biased person can also rely on others to assume responsibility. Sometimes this overwhelming need for others can lead to neurosis and regression to earlier states of personal development. Neurosis can often find itself present in the next camp—the enmeshed.

Everyone has been in this camp of the biased at one time or another. At birth everyone is exclusively a resident of this camp, since infants are totally dependent on others for their survival. A person in his early years relies on mother to feed, clothe, and secure him. Although many adults do not need these basic physical needs, they are psychologically dependent on others for their needs. The biased, and especially the narcissist, can also be likened to an astronomical phenomenon—a black hole. These entities in outer space have such great gravity that even light itself cannot escape their grasp. This is much like the biased, who say, "It is all about me," "My wants, my needs," "Give me, give me." As the black hole sucks the energy out of a star or other heavenly bodies, the biased suck the energy out of people. But, I hope, most people can overcome this state of selfishness to become a more fully functional being; however, many people vacillate from this camp to other camps.

The best example of the biased person is the person who, at a party, is the first to talk about himself. Indeed, it is human nature to want to be understood and in some cases to be the center of attention, but the biased is the first to tell another about his accomplishments and interests. Once others take their turn to talk about themselves, the biased will become uninterested, unless by listening, they can gain something toward themselves. Of all of the camps, the biased understand the authentic concept of love the least.

THE ENMESHED

This camp is home to the neurotics and codependents. Much like the biased, the enmeshed are like black holes, with the distinction that the enmeshed are black holes who find other black holes to mutually suck one another's energy away. In this seductive dance, the two enmeshed find a downward spiral of negativism and at times even destruction.

Once there was a young woman, who through a life of substance abuse and self-destruction (cutting) found a friend at a local bar, who had a life similar to her own. At a young age both of these women had been physically abused, and both of them had in turn been adopted through foster care. Both had led a life of self-mutilation, which led them to residential treatment. The two instantly "hit it off." Soon both of them were calling each other to go out to coffee and to double date. They began to talk about going into business with one another. Both of the women were into the "punk" scene and felt like they should design their own line of clothing in a unique style. After a short while, both of the women were seeing each other two, three, four times per day. They began to talk about the "old life" and started glorifying their old drug use. Slowly, meeting for coffee became meeting for marijuana, and then meeting for marijuana became meeting for heroin. As both of them slid down the path of self-destruction, one of the women's therapists began to become aware of the relapses and advised her to stop the relationship. This created a response of "I don't have a problem and if I did, she has nothing to do with it." They had both become two black holes, stealing each other's light and following a path of annihilation.

Oftentimes, the enmeshed can be much more subtle than the above example, such as the father and son who need to spend all of their free time with each other because they are filling the void of their lost mother and spouse. They become psychically tied to one another, and a split can cause high levels of anxiety.

The enmeshed can be explained further by exploring the binary-orbital distortions found among them, which in some ways relate to the psycho-analytic concepts of transference (emotional reactions that are assigned to current relationships but originated in earlier experiences) added to the concept of parataxic distortions (inaccurate perceptions an individual has about actions, feelings, thoughts, and motives of those with whom emotional relationships are found). However, binary-orbital distortions exist only in a one-on-one relationship. These distortions are parataxic distortions, which are mutually shared. Although shared delusions can affect a group of religious zealots, who, for example, believe that their leader is a god (such as the David Koresh clan of Waco, Texas, in the 1990s), those who have a binary-orbital distortion share almost identically the same distortion with one other person. These distortions can only be found among the enmeshed, because there must be no more than two who share these distortions. Binary-orbital distortions can be synonymous with mutual obsession.

Many times among the enmeshed these binary-orbital distortions are mistaken for love. Statements such as "You complete me," or "I can't live without you" are in essence binary-orbital distortions, because they show a surrendering of oneself exclusively to the needs of another. Again, the previous statements must be shared between the enmeshed for it to be a binary-orbital distortion. These feelings may be felt as authentic, but often they are misguided notions of reality.

Those in this camp can experience authentic love; however, their binary-orbital distortions are so severe that the two individuals become "glued" to each other and cannot function outside of that union. Essentially, they become a selfish "one," and their union is an alliance of mutually shared object interest. Many abusive relationships stem from this type of relationship. If we consider the Drama Triangle, we can find the victim, rescuer, and the persecutor of this triangle within this camp.

Persons who experience authentic love transcend the Drama Triangle, because they have the self-respect to not be the victim, they are assertive enough to stand up to the persecutor, they are compassionate enough to not oppress, and they are independent enough to not make excuses to rescue or collude. If they have been exposed

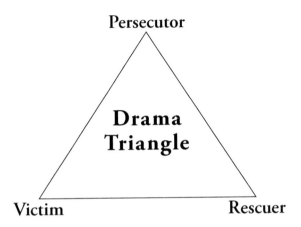

to a traumatic event, these individuals, through an understanding of choice with willingness to take charge of their lives, become survivors of the trauma. They understand that past trauma can have a profound influence on their lives, but they are not determined or controlled by this trauma.

Before we move on to the next camp, this would be an opportune time to introduce the following chart, the Hierarchy of Human Needs:

A Hierarchy of Human Needs

1. Survival
2. Safety
3. Touching, skin contact
4. Attention
5. Mirroring and echoing
6. Guidance
7. Listening
8. Being real
9. Participating
10. Acceptance
11. Opportunity to grieve and grow
12. Support
13. Loyalty and trust
14. Accomplishment
15. Altering state of consciousness
16. Sexuality
17. Enjoyment of fun
18. Freedom
19. Nurturing
20. Self-actualization[1]

As we search these camps, we can see that each of these human needs can fit into each camp as a person's character develops.

Now consider, if number 1 (survival) and number 2 (safety) are not being fulfilled in a person's life, all of the other needs will not be met, because the individual is focused primarily on getting these two needs met. Indeed, guidance, listening, and enjoyment of fun cannot be fulfilled if a person is starving and searching for the next meal.

The biased and the enmeshed live their lives desperately seeking the first ten needs found on this list. They are obsessed with being accepted and finding guidance and attention. Their belief is that they are barely surviving. Their belief that the world is not a safe place stifles their growth, and they live a life stuck in a negative cycle of toxic guilt and shame.

As we consider the camp "self-objectivist," it will be discovered that these individuals have fulfilled many of the lower ten human needs on this scale and are actively engaged in fulfilling the remaining ten.

THE SELF-OBJECTIVIST

The narcissists can have their feet placed in this camp as well as in the camp of the biased and enmeshed, but they cannot maintain this camp for long. This state is inhabited and maintained by independent people who are emotionally mature and in many ways have climbed to the top of the hierarchy of human needs to become "self-actualized," or have achieved a full development of potentials (but only in the scope of an individual's self). Whereas the biased and the enmeshed are fixated in lower stages of development—physiological needs, safety needs, needs of belonging, and so on—the self-objectivists may have found balance in their lives. Many of society's leaders are found among the self-objectivists, but this camp can be lonely as well.

For example, Sarah's life was a life of organization and ambitions. She had graduated at the top of her class from a prestigious Ivy League university. Through self-discipline and down-and-dirty hard work, she had made her little start-up company into a Fortune 500 organization. Sarah had three houses, a private jet, and millions of dollars. She would date from time to time, but would say, "Relationships take too much effort . . . besides I need to focus on what is important in life, my career." Eventually, Sarah was married to a wealthy engineer. However, Sarah started to wonder, "Why do I feel empty? I have played all of the right cards." Sarah had met all of the goals that she had set out for herself to accomplish since college. She even had a good heart and would often donate large amounts of money to charities. Wasn't this who she was supposed to be? Western society would define Sarah's life as an ultimate success, so why did her misery eventually lead her to find answers through psychoanalysis and quick-fix self-actualization seminars?

Was it because her relationship with her father was a relationship of ambivalence, and because of object loss, through the death of a loved one at an early age, she had intellectualized and sublimated her life, as her analyst claimed? She was an independent person and many people aspired to be like her, so what was the answer to her predicament? Or maybe there wasn't one.

The self-objectivists are definitely more psychically and socially mature than the biased and the enmeshed. The self-objectivists have achieved formal reasoning and mature thought, and much of their cognition (thought) is in line with the folkways and mores (traditions and rules) of the established norms. They also have a smaller amount of thought distortions than do the biased and the enmeshed, because they can conceptualize outside of themselves or their immediate other. Indeed, this mature cognition is more complex than the abstract manipulations that are part of the repertoire of the biased and enmeshed. Cognition with the self-objectivist is flexible, open, and adaptable, unlike the dichotomous, all-or-nothing thoughts and attitudes of the previous two camps. Moreover, the self-objectivist can at times function in the emotional realm and intellectual realm of thought and affect simultaneously, thus having a more objective view of reality. The previous two camps vacillate between extreme emotion and intellectualization, which often is the causal factor in acute thought distortions.

The emotional and cognitive functioning of the self-objectivist is post-formal in nature, meaning that as self-objectivists deal with a chaotic world, they rely on subjective experience and intuitions as well as logic as navigators. They can deal with ambiguity, uncertainty, inconsistency, contradiction, imperfection, and compromise. Indeed, unlike the previous two camps, the self-objectivist can see the grays of reality and does not think in terms of black and white (right versus wrong, intellect versus feelings).

As we can see, the self-objectivist can be a "self-actualized" individual, having overcome many of the dependent needs of the biased and

41

enmeshed. However, as we will see, the self-objectivists can be in touch with authentic loving but have a difficult time maintaining it because of their nature of being "independent"—or focusing on the "one."

THE VILLAGER

This is the community-oriented person, who is interdependent and realizes that he needs himself and others to get what they both need and want. Villagers understand that they can stand alone but prefer to have a relationship with others to strive to find unity in balance. As with the self-objectivist, the villager is a self-actualized individual; however, actualization doesn't exist within the villager, but actualization occurs with others in the villager's life—self-actualization becomes community actualization.

Both the self-objectivist and the villager experience authentic loving at times; however, the villager often experiences true love at an exponentially greater rate than does the self-objectivist, because the villager's understanding of reality often exists outside of his own need.

In discussions one and two, the example of the classic love story was told. The young man and woman run into each other at a corner market and fall instantly and madly in love with one another. The question was asked: "Why didn't their relationship work?" The answer is in a greater understanding of the difference between the self-objectivist and the villager. In this fictional story, both of these people were independent individuals. They both held good jobs and both wanted much of the same things from life: security, money, family, happiness. They seemingly had a strong foundation built on the ideals that were taught to them from an early age. So why didn't the marriage take? Many individuals are like these two people.

Whereas the biased was likened to a black hole and the enmeshed could be two black holes sucking energy from one another, the villager is like a binary star, in orbit around another. Independently, each member of the binary system has an actualized amount of its own energy; however, through its unity the system has even greater power and mutually benefits the other and the universe around it. Many marriages are based on either the enmeshed, self-objectivists, or villagers. The villagers are those who succeed, for they are built on mutual benefit and selfless action. But the villager even goes beyond this, for the villager is not only interdependent with a significant other but also interdependent with his or her ecology. Even in a great union of support between two people, authentic loving can be lost when the union attempts to achieve love exclusively in the realm of that union. Authentic love must occur outside the one, and many times "the one" is the union, because the couple has become united. And authentic love does occur outside unions, with those who at times do not reciprocate the love from the individual or the union. For example, the villager will be selfless even toward those who are selfish, like the narcissists.

When there is no reward for a good deed with the exception of furthering love, you will find the villager and also the universalist, which I will discuss in the next camp. The villager at times realizes this and has a greater understanding that the community is interrelated and what affects one part of the community, among one union or relationship, affects the whole community.

Thus, we can see that the classic love story could not succeed in the realm of the union because the two individuals were only thinking of their own individual needs and at times within only their union or relationship. The conceptions possessed by the villager were not part of their schema and values, thus the union itself dissolved; the union, or the relationship, was not supported by the mutual energy of the community, nor possibly was it even allowed in the relationship.

In a marriage between villagers, the community is still current within the couple's hearts. The needs of the community are of important to the couple, which negates isolation within the union. Oftentimes, individuals get "stuck in the rut" of daily living—get up, go to work, come home, watch some television, go to sleep—they are satisfied and comfortable in a life of mutual isolation with each other. As the husband and wife become one through matrimony, they feel that they have arrived. "Why concern myself with others? I have my one true love and a couple of kids on the way." They forget, or were never even aware, that they live in an ecology, where one action affects other actions and outcomes. If one couple begins to fall into mutual narcissism, the community might follow, and a status quo of narcissism will be established in that community.

The villager is aware of the fact that an individual must be active in the community and break the bonds of mutual narcissism found within many unions of people. Being active beyond one mutual relationship will bring energy and constant rejuvenation to that very relationship.

And that union will be actively participating continuously in authentic loving of others.

The Universalist

Universalists transcend the limits of being placed in a camp; it would be more appropriate to put them in a league. These individuals have realized the vicissitudes of others and are oriented toward the "brotherhood of mankind." They have realized a spiritual side through love—the love that comes from serving others. They are extrinsic-interdependent, relying on the spiritual side of their nature. These individuals would be associated with other titles such as solitary, sojourner, or even saint. They can be in tune with what is known as "essence" which is synonymous with no-mind (existential), suchness (Zen), the eternal now, or God's will. Essence is essentially a state of mind in which a person experiences love in its basic form, that of love in balance, love in synthesis, beyond the black and white, beyond the dichotomous notions of this or that. The universalist feels this in-tunement, or at-one-ment, for the universalist has passed through the other previously mentioned camps and has gained an understanding of his own awareness of self, others, environment, and the universe. The Universalist experiences transcendence of the usual perceptions of alienation and isolation, and this comes as a unifying experience achieved through union with other people, nature, knowledge, religion, and so forth. Indeed, the universalist may feel rooted in a divine communion. The true Universalists are in and of themselves authentic love, for they are full of the action of love, or charity. Universalists not only operate in the realm of relationships between, but they also operate in relationships without. They are not merely in relationship with a spouse, a friend, a community, an ecology, but the universe.

The universalists are individuals who are active with CORE, as it applies to authentic love. CORE is an acronym representing: Cohesiveness (or balance), Orientation (or awareness), Resiliency, and an understanding of the Existential. CORE will be addressed in more detail in later discussions. Sufficient for our current discussion, CORE is essentially the universalists themselves, for they are balanced in their perceptions of reality as they choose to understand the synthesis (the grays) in life, not the dichotomies (blacks and whites) of life. The universalist is also active in pursuing self-awareness. Through self-awareness, a greater understanding and wisdom of truth and authentic love can be conceptualized. And to be a universalist, we must realize acceptance by simply existing as we are.

NOTE

1. Abraham Maslow, *Motivation and Personality* (New York: Harper, 1954), 236.

Discussion 5

PAIN, DREAD, AND SUFFERING

FDR said, " We have nothing to fear, but fear itself" . . . Perhaps it needs to be modified to " We have nothing to fear . . . Period."
—Anonymous

MOTHER TERESA STATED, "IN THE SLUMS, in the broken body, in the children, we see Christ and we touch him."[1] The true understanding of suffering and dread are found through the existential, the spiritual, and authentic love. The Western world's notion of pain is a simple misunderstanding that pain is only suffering, the opposite of pleasure, and that it affords us no redeeming value.

There are two forms of dread, the one negative and painful, and the other positive, loving, and enlightening. The non-enlightened evoking reaction is experienced as fear, anxiety, depression, outrage, despair, and isolation. The enlightened evoking reaction is seen as unity, union, compassion, charity, humor, awe, and peace. The universalist looks pain, suffering, and dread in the face, and instead of running away, as would those in other camps, the universalist chooses not to ignore or deny it.

Through exposure to suffering and dread, the universalist has become aware of a basic form of wisdom—pure empathy. Realistically, most individuals will not always respond to pain with joy and acceptance, especially those who have been exposed to the Western notions of these concepts, for it is difficult to not want to take the path of least resistance and try to find pleasure over pain. The learning and wisdom that comes from exposure to pain and suffering can help an individual grow exponentially. Buddha professed that suffering came from three destructive states: greed, anger, and destructive delusions. In the camps of the enmeshed or biased, pain can actually cause regression. The enmeshed and the biased see dread, pain, and suffering as roadblocks to their narcissistic needs.

For example, to narcissists, a car accident that results in the loss of a limb can destroy their overinflated and distorted sense of self; they might say, "I am not a whole person anymore, because without my looks, I am nothing!" If this individual does not have a strong paradigm shift, or shift in global perspective, he may find himself in the darkest recesses of despair and anguish. However, if this person can leap to another camp and change his perspective toward the injury, he might find an abundant source of wisdom resulting from the accident. He might receive a higher level of empathy toward others who have been through a similar circumstance, or he may even begin to understand the human condition through pure empathy.

Empathy can be achieved by traveling many paths, and many people possess empathy for certain circumstances or individuals in their lives. Empathy is defined as the act of perceiving, understanding, experiencing, and responding to the emotional state and ideas of another person. However, empathy can be limited because all of us position ourselves in our own reality. So how can we really, truly understand the position of another? Our lives are painted by our experiences and circumstances, and, in many ways, our realms of perception parallel many others' perceptions.

I remember when I was an adolescent, I thought no one understood me. I thought I was alone in this world. This created fear, because I believed "if no one understands, then I am not safe in taking chances, especially social chances." As I grew older and my understanding became refined, I began to realize that many other people had similar thoughts and feelings to mine; perhaps others would understand. These ideas led to a lessening of fear and an increased bonding with my fellow beings.

Even at this stage in my life, I knew that others might feel the way that I did about circumstances and situations. Out of my own perspectives, which I assumed to be similar to others' perspectives, I could respond to the emotional states and ideas of others because these states were similar to my own. With this blueprint, I could pattern a strategy of responses to address the needs of others. Yet how could I truly and deeply understand a greater number of people without first going through similar experiences? Without these experiences, could I really understand other individuals' positions? Indeed, I could empathize with others, but without the ingredient of pure empathy, I could not reach the core of the other individual.

Pure empathy is found in the realm of authentic loving, and as stated previously, it is a trait of the universalist. Pure empathy can only be found through the spiritual realm. Perhaps the only way to understand it is through the writings of those who have been in possession of it. But the only way to gain the deepest understanding of it—meaning having wisdom about it—is to travel a road through pain and dread, and overcome suffering and fear by accepting these realities.

Let us now gain some insight into pure empathy by exploring the writings of those who have been exposed to and embraced suffering in order to overcome it:

Suffering brings forth affirming acceptance—affirming life situations in spite of painful complications. Take for example Job in the Old Testament. Throughout his life, Job lived in comfort and great riches; however, even though he had material wealth, his personal strength was built upon his core values, principles, and, most important, his spirituality. Job's spiritual perspective helped him overcome pain and suffering; even when he lost all, he did not alter his character:

"Then Job arose, and rent his mantle, and shaved his head, and fell down upon the ground, and worshipped, and said, Naked came I out of my mother's womb, and naked shall I return thither: the Lord gave, and the Lord hath taken away; blessed be the name of the Lord" (Job 1:20–22).

And because Job transcended his suffering, he grew in spiritual strength and gained a broader understanding and wisdom: "When he has tried me, I shall come forth as gold" (Job 23:10).

Overcoming pain and suffering leads an individual to a greater understanding of life and a greater understanding of the human condition, which leads to pure empathy or "God's perspective."

Why do individuals suffer? An answer to this cannot be found in the general idea of empathy, but in the higher understanding of pure empathy. We suffer, as individuals, as people, as a society *because* of our perspectives. Our personal intelligences and our sensations and perceptions deceive us into a belief of the dualism of self and others; we are led to act as though we are separate, as I truly believed as an adolescent—that I was alone and that no one understood me. Even now, my own perceptions fool me into thinking that I am "I" and that all others are "they." "I" becomes fixated in many individuals' lives: "This is mine," "I own this," "This is yours," and so on. Through a study of Zen training, one learns that many of these notions are set up by what is called ego (this is different from the ego in psychoanalytic writing). Ego in Zen essentially means the same as narcissism, or the focus on self, me, or "I." Even in Zen thought, the term egocentrism means the focus and enlargement of oneself. Essentially, the Zen notion of ego is similar to the idea of the natural man, who is an enemy of God.

To better understand these concepts, it would be effective to synthesize the psychic development attributed to psychodynamic thought with the Zen idea of Ego and then add upon it. The following discussion will be an elaboration of the diagram below:

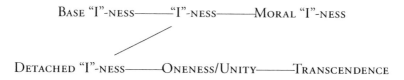

BASE "I"-NESS————"I"-NESS————MORAL "I"-NESS

DETACHED "I"-NESS————ONENESS/UNITY————TRANSCENDENCE

Base "I"-ness is much like Freud's concept of id but has many differences. It contains everything that is inherited and instinctual. Base "I"-ness is found with the birth of the individual; the infant's life consists of instant gratification. According to Freud, there are no anxieties or conflicts tied to the id; this is the same with base "I"-ness. Contradictions, dichotomies, and antitheses exist side by side, but in an immature manner, unlike that of higher developmental thought. Since the infant has this attribute, the base "I"-ness forms the core of our being. And yet base "I"-ness is ultimately selfish, for it has no concept of the external world—even a child's perception of mother is consumed by inaccessible selfishness, for the infant's perception of mother is essentially a perception of an object of self-gratification. Again, base "I"-ness knows of no anxiety, because a higher concept of the external world must be integrated for anxiety to occur; this is the job of "I"-ness. However, *fear* does exist at this level.

(Before we move on, it must be emphasized that through this exploration of certain concepts of psychodynamics, the theories described will only be used as a guide to understand suffering and, ultimately, the concept of love. As one studies the theories of Freud, one comes to realize that his theories are based on the concept of psychic determinism, or essentially, the idea that the individual is determined to be a certain way because of psychic phenomena [conscious, pre-conscious, and unconscious]; little emphasis is placed on personal choice. We must realize that our lives are only determined by our agency—or the choices we make. If an individual wholly ascribes his actions to Freud's theories, then ultimately personal responsibility does not exist. This is a dangerous and destructive concept, and we will explore this further in a later discussion.)

"I"-ness comes at a much later stage of life than does base "I"-ness. It differentiates itself in function. As the psychodynamic concept of ego acts as a reality test and mediator between the id and the super-ego, "I"-ness mediates the base "I"-ness from the moral "I"-ness. However, "I"-ness is purely subjective. Although the external world informs "I"-ness, this state interprets the external to its own experience and because of its modifications of the external world to its own advantage, the "I"-ness will ultimately lead back to the internal functioning of the individual. The "I"-ness component of us is both the product of our inner psyche and our society.

Our culture is indoctrinated by the idea of "me" and "mine." Even in our speech we use many possessive pronouns, which add to this distorted reality. Thus, unlike Freud's claim that the ego is the seat of reality, the idea of "I"-ness is attributed to non-reality, because its focus is only on itself and not the "other"—on subjective rather than objective—as essentially is psycho-analytic's ego.

"I"-ness is indeed a relay station between base "I"-ness and moral "I"-ness, and though it finds itself in pure subjectiveness, it can lead to a path of objective reality and even transcendence. As we consider the above diagram, we see that through "I"-ness, we can detach and let go of our subjective self and find ourselves in a state of detached "I"-ness (this will be discussed in more detail momentarily). For our current discussion, we need to realize that "I"-ness can lead us through many doors.

For most people, "I"-ness leads to the emergence of moral "I"-ness, or a "subjective society ideal." This is an interesting personality component, because on the one hand it is totally informed by the environment; however, it also distorts objectivity and develops personal rigid truth. Unlike base "I"-ness, which knows no dichotomies, moral "I"-ness is bombarded with dichotomies—right and wrong, black and white, good and evil—and these polar cognitions and feelings can be very destructive, for they can become part of one's subjective truth, which leads to personal rigidity.

An example of "I"-ness is a person with whom the mores of society must be upheld at all costs. These individuals want justice and penalty with little consideration for mercy. Intolerance is a calling card of moral "I"-ness. In Dostoevsky's classic *The Grand Inquisitor*, we find an individual who possesses, or is possessed and controlled by, his moral "I"-ness. *The Grand Inquisitor* is the story of a cardinal who views everyone with rigid concreteness, for he believes that all should be made obedient, without free will, and through this view he professes that his subjugation is done through the will of the Lord, or for *ad majorem gloriam Dei*—"the greater glory of God"—the Jesuit motto. When the grand inquisitor is confronted by the Lord Himself, the cardinal plans to burn the Lord as "the greatest heretic" because the Lord has come back to change the status quo once more.[2]

The individual possessed of moral "I"-ness is no lover of freedom and revels in the status quo. However, moral "I"-ness is not always a negative function of our personality, as long as it is not the overwhelming influence upon our personality. For example, we all need to live in a society of laws and ascribe to those laws a good majority of the time, or else chaos will run rampant, and anomie (a collapse of social structure) could take hold. And truly, mercy cannot rob justice.

Moral "I"-ness is usually developed through guilt experiences as an individual matures. For example, if a child is punished and shamed throughout his life, without any positive reinforcement, that child develops into a person who punishes and shames. This child will develop a moral compass focused on desires to gain approval of those who shamed him or her. However, moral "I"-ness can be functional; it can develop judgments based on the upholding of laws to maintain social order.

Considering the previous diagram, an awareness is highlighted in that "I"-ness leads to moral "I"-ness, but it is also a conduit toward *detached "I"-ness*.

In considering what *detached "I"-ness* could mean, we must think outside of ourselves—for this is essentially what detached "I"-ness is—"thinking outside of ourselves." Detached "I"-ness is the same as the idea of *not "I,"* the idea of discontinuing the focus of self-identity, which would truly be beyond the scope of the "I"-ness. The detached "I"-ness occurs in many people's lives as they render service to others. In that moment of acting outside of oneself, one can detach from identity interests and focus more on the community. The villager spends the majority of his or her time in this state—actually, detached "I"-ness and the camp of the villager are almost the same concept, except the former is a state of personality and the latter is more a state of being.

Oneness/Unity is similar to detached "I"-ness in that it can also be found when a person serves others; however, as an individual separates from self in detached "I"-ness, oneness and unity then reincorporate self into a union with others—a type of interdependence. This state is where one would find a person who is concerned about the ecology of life—he realizes that all things are united and affect one another. Again, the villager roams in this state, for the villager is aware of the effects he has on the community and environment and how these entities in turn affect them villagers in a profound way.

Notwithstanding what has been said of oneness/unity, this state of personality is better defined as the mortar between detached "I"-ness and transcendence, because it glues the two of these states together—or oneness/unity is the step that one takes from being a villager to being a universalist; we shall soon see why.

Transcendence is consistent with the idea of truly being the total activity of all forms in a given situation and not being at the same moment. And subject and object are the same. Everything within and without the personality is happening at once, yet is not. In Zen Buddhism this personality state would somewhat correlate with what is called "Satori" or a moment of supreme enlightenment, yet transcendence is usually maintained by the individual or becomes incorporated into personality.

Another way of looking at transcendence is to see the world with ultimate acceptance. This is the way Christ saw the world, with ultimate acceptance, with unconditional love. This personality state is possessed by the universalist.

Transcendence is a difficult state to arrive at (and almost impossible to maintain), for one must pass through many of the other states, detach from self, unify with others, and then reincorporate a "new" self-interdependence with all others and God. This can only be accomplished through suffering, which suffering brings acceptance, which acceptance brings forth love. It can only be found once an individual has let go and found atonement through repentance. The transcendence that is attached to acceptance, which brings forth love, is only found in the repentant moment of loss and despair that prepares the detached "I"-ness to experience the profound ideal of acceptance and pure empathy that leads to love.

Pain must happen because it leads to a better understanding of love. And it is through pain that we have the opportunity to change, and change brings growth. Essentially, an individual's perspective of pain, or the way in which someone stands outside (in perspective) of pain is what leads to suffering. But you may ask, "Why must I experience pain to grow?" A believer of Christ might grapple with the question, "Why did God the Father send his Only Begotten Son to this world to expose him to so much pain and suffering?" People who believe in the ideas of God's will, or to a lesser extent "karma," are not compelled to ask these questions.

One notion that runs through many religious ideas and even through much current psychotherapy is the concept of acceptance, or as it is referred to in dialectical behavioral therapy, "radical acceptance." The true definition of acceptance is an understanding of the core of causation and the primary and secondary causes that arise, and then seeing the effects that these causes perpetuate. And even beyond the causes and effects, we can see our participation in all of it. We can then understand that we are responsible, and if responsible, that we can do something about it.

NOTES

1. Muggeridge, M., *Something Beautiful for God* (San Francisco: Harper and Row, 1971). Quoted in Gantt, "Hedonism, Suffering, and Redemption," 53.

2. F. Dostoevsky, *The Grand Inquisitor,* e-book (Public Domain Books, 2004).

Discussion 6

SACRIFICE

---

*For whosoever will save his life shall lose it: But whosoever will
lose his life for my sake, the same shall save it.*
                                                    —Luke 9:24

NOW THAT A GREATER UNDERSTANDING OF pain and dread has been
realized, let us look closer at what keeps an individual from succumbing to pain—which succumbing can bring suffering—and explore
how we can gain pure empathy and obtain the state of mind known
as *essence*.

The simple but ultimate answer is that individuals must sacrifice. An
individual who has experienced transcendence understands the need for
sacrifice as much as the need to transcend suffering and pain.

The greatest loving comes through sacrifice, and the best example of
this is the love between parents and children. What a sacrifice it is to give
away ego interest, narcissistic desires of financial comfort, and the acquisition of things for a child.

"But why sacrifice in the first place? What is in it for me?" These questions are ideas of the biased and the narcissist, whose thoughts dwell only
on their own gratification and fulfillment. These statements are not built
on the principle and action of love.

And how does one get in touch with pure empathy? By walking on
the dark roads of others who suffer, those who have searched out the spiritual through their pain by sacrificing a part of themselves—this is pure
empathy. For it to be a sacrifice, it must have some level of pain.

The rich philanthropist who donates thousands from his millions of
dollars to a charity has not really sacrificed, but the single mother who

sells her last piece of jewelry to support her religion has truly sacrificed—this is the "widow's mite."

A rich young ruler asked Jesus, "What shall I do to inherit eternal life?" Christ answered, "Thou knowest the commandments, do not commit adultery, do not kill, do not steal, do not bear false witness, honor thy father and thy mother." And the rich ruler responded, "All these have I kept from my youth." When Jesus heard this, he said, "Yet lackest thou one thing: sell all that thou hast, and distribute unto the poor, and thou shalt have treasure in heaven" (see Luke 19:20–22). In his narcissism, the ruler rejected these words because his material was too precious to him, even more precious than eternal life!

Sacrifice brings convictions and greater wisdom into a person's spiritual self. When an individual sacrifices, it brings with it some pain—pain for whatever is being removed and sacrificed—but through the pain comes greater understanding and awareness of joy. This is an idea that is lacking in many conventional modes of psychotherapy . . . to truly elevate pain isn't to mask it or avoid it, but to work through it and be mindful of it. An understanding of pain and sacrifice could be made with the simple example of exercise. Workouts such as cardiovascular training can be rigorous and painful, but once the routines are finished, a person can increase in esteem and satisfaction because of work accomplished and the increase in both health and wellness.

The above examples may explain the dire circumstances in which our society now finds itself. Because of the way people avoid, it can be seen that suffering is only exacerbated. Pain-avoiding coping strategies are these: substance abuse, overeating, idleness, excessive entertainment, self-mutilation, any addiction, pornography, eating disorders, excessive spending, and so on. Anything that leads one closer to hedonism and narcissism and further away from growth is a pain-avoidant strategy. Yet the more an individual sacrifices these base desires of consumption and avoidance, the more the individual grows, develops, and transcends.

Pain avoidance leads to stagnation and even regression. Anyone who has known or worked with someone who is dependent on drugs could attest to the fact that when an individual begins to use substances to avoid pain, that person then becomes fixated at the age when he began to use.

For example, I worked with one individual who began using substances at the age of thirteen. This person was twenty-three when I began to work with him, yet emotionally he was still thirteen. He lost ten years of emotional maturity, and his perceptions were those of the biased, for he was plagued with notions of self-gratification and neurotic tendencies. Yet another example was a thirty-year-old woman who began self-mutilation at the age of sixteen; not only did she fixate at the age of sixteen, but she also regressed emotionally to the age of six or younger. Her thinking became preoccupied with concrete operations of dichotomies, for she saw life as all or nothing, black and white, ultimate good or ultimate evil.

The motivation to avoid this world of pain and suffering and discover one of greater harmony, joy, and meaning, triggers most addictions. Resorting to mind-altering drugs, for example, corresponds to a frantic and compelling attempt to experience feelings at a deep level and to overcome the lack of ability to love, which is rooted in a materialistic, fear-ridden, dehumanized society with its focus on hedonism. However, like anything in life, there are no shortcuts; mind-altering drugs are tied to a narcissistic society and instead of escaping the pain, an individual is brought to a full recollection and awareness of the pain once the drug is taken away. And in fact, the person is in further bondage to the materialistic society.

Sacrifice can be an agent for change or a way for an individual to heal. To regain control—once control has been lost to an addiction—and to progress rapidly from years of emotional and existential fixation and regression, takes discipline. And to turn from an old life of self-interest and excessive consumption takes sacrifice.

But how does one practice discipline to increase sacrifice? The word *discipline* has a bad connotation because of the way Western society has viewed it as the opposite of pleasure, full of rigidness, authoritarianism, and hostility. In reality, discipline is the first step toward joy. Having a productive, scheduled day leads to fulfillment. Personal vision and management leads to an increasingly productive life, which leads to fulfillment, which leads to joy. But it must be realized that discipline must be intrinsically motivated and not externally exerted on an individual. It must be a person's choice to live a life of structure, and only then will the perception of discipline be seen as pleasant.

In many ways discipline is the only way to overcome addictions. Essentially, addictions are merely overindulgence; this is especially true for a dependence on a substance, be it drugs or food. Indeed, discipline is the underlying focus of any twelve-step program. The person who was once addicted must practice sobriety day by day, being mindful of cravings and triggers, having a self-awareness of personal vulnerabilities. These individuals must cognitively map out every aspect of their addiction, either mentally or visually on paper; if for one moment they lose focus and vision, then relapse becomes likely.

Indeed, every individual must learn self-discipline; this is how we grow. Being mindful of our thoughts and feelings, analyzing our own behavior to keep us aligned with our personal goals, takes concentration and patience.

To arrive at an intrinsic level of self-discipline and at transcendence, we must ultimately sacrifice our own carnal desires. The individual who is addicted must suspend his will to the will of God. An individual needs to follow a pattern that Christ set: "[Jesus] kneeling down, prayed, saying, Father, if thou be willing, remove this cup from me: nevertheless not my will, but thine, be done" (Luke 22:41–42). Seeking the will of God and striving to see others as God sees them—this is pure empathy! And it will lead to the state of Essence, or being one with the Creator.

Discussion 7

CHARITY

And now abideth faith, hope, charity, these three; but the greatest of these is charity.

—1 Corinthians 13:12

Repentance can be a harsh word to some, but it is necessary to transcend. Historically, the word has been associated with the terms *unrighteous force, coercion,* and *domination.* However, repentance is essentially freedom—freedom from guilt, shame, and uncleanliness. Repentance helps one reach atonement (at-one-ment)—or wholeness.

The repentance process is actually the abandonment of the narcissistic aspects of self. An individual loses his old self, and in this very moment of loss, when an individual gains a sense of healthy shame and healthy guilt, he experiences a profound acceptance—affirmation. Repentance is the very opposite of piety or righteous indignation. It is, however, an experience of humility, a recognition of one's own "unworthiness." At this moment of humility, one's worthiness appears.

The Jewish existentialist Martin Buber speaks of repentance as "turning." It is turning from an experience of the world from the "I-It" perception, where all forms are objects to be manipulated, to the "I-Thou" perception, where every experience offers relationship, opportunities, and the potential for contact with others and the Infinite. Repentance is truly acceptance—acceptance that we are human, that we make mistakes, that through communion with a higher power and by utilizing the grace and sacrifice of Christ, we can overcome, we can be made whole, and that we are "okay."

Now let us talk more about love: The thing about love is that you can't taste it, you can't kinetically feel it, you can't smell it, you can't hear it, you can't see it with visual senses. So how do you know that it is there? How can you describe it, and how do you know others feel it in the same qualitative way that you do?

Like gravity, you can't see the phenomenon, but you know of its presence, for everything around it is affected by it. This is much like love; the evidence of its existence is found in the virtues that surround it. One of these virtues is compassion. This aspect of love is a quintessential ingredient needed for every individual to overcome the narcissistic self. The object interest turned inward begins to diminish as awareness and sense of unity with the community and humankind begins to increase.

This virtue of loving is synonymous with charity. But how does one acquire compassion and charity? How does one transcend the narcissist? Perhaps by defining compassion and charity the answer will appear: compassion is the antithesis of narcissism.

God created this world to be a place of finite forms, which would enable us to experience love. Without the frailties of this world, there could be no love. Love takes many forms: care, compassion, conflict, creativity, appreciation, joy, grief, and forgiveness.

Paul the apostle of Christ wrote, "Charity suffereth long, and is kind; charity envieth not; charity vaunteth not itself, is not puffed up, doth not behave itself unseemingly, seeketh not her own, is not easily provoked, thinketh no evil; rejoiceth not in iniquity, but rejoices in truth; beareth all things, believeth all things, endureth all things . . . charity never faileth" (1 Corinthians 13:4–8).

CORE
TRANSFORMATION

CORE TRANSFORMATION IS ESSENTIALLY A FOCUS on the core of the being. What makes up each individual's core? The relationships we have with others influence our core. Our values and character are something we need to be aware of to help ourselves overcome negative influences in our environment. And we need to have an understanding of our spirituality to transcend existential angst.

CORE transformation is identified as such to distinguish it from merely being a type of "therapy." The term *transformation* is deliberately used because unlike therapy, this dialogue can take place both in the office of a therapist/interviewer and can be used in any relationship. It is also referred to as a "transformation" because through the sessions or interviews, the relationship between interviewer and the participant is evolving and growing in tandem. The idea of the all-knowing therapist, teacher, parent, or spouse is replaced with the concept of a dialogue occurring between two equals whose purpose is to gain greater awareness and growth in spiritual, relational, emotional, philosophical, attitudinal, behavioral, and cognitive areas of the self.

To those seeking therapy: As a person seeks a therapist, that person must consider the fact that healing only takes place when a relationship has been established. I have found that the following characteristics—which will be described as CORE—are essential characteristics leading to healing. I seek these traits in therapists from whom I want help. If you are looking for a therapist, seek an individual who exhibits aspects of the characteristics that will be described in this section. It will make a world of difference!

Discussion 8

COHESIVENESS

To mind and mental inquires do acquire but little . . . The heart inspires to overcome the trivial! And know not these people who are so like ourselves intellectual, but the wise mind understands all!

—Anonymous

FOR AN INTERVIEWER, COHESIVENESS MEANS BEING one with the person the interviewer is helping. This can come in the form of authenticity—being interested and having a profound respect for those whom you help. For a moment, think back to a time when you were smitten with someone. What was that like? Do you remember that communication? Time didn't seem to have any meaning; the world around you disappeared—this is cohesive communication, or soul talk. It is called soul talk, because at a crucial moment, the environment disappears, and you are totally immersed in the insight of another person. You are not just talking, but your spirits are touching (ultimately aware, interested, and respectful). You are hypnotized by the details of the other person.

Interpersonal cohesiveness is in a way like observing each other gaining insight—and what a transpersonal experience it is. As a therapist, I must reach this level of communication with my clients. Of course, a client-therapist relationship is not the same as a relationship between lovers, but the two share some similarities. For in what other relationships do you get to such a level of intimacy than with a spouse, a family member, or a therapist? However, unlike a spouse or family member, a therapist must be *ultimately concerned, but unconcerned ultimately*—a conundrum meaning that a therapist must be able to achieve interpersonal cohesiveness, but be able to detach once the client has exited the session. If this detachment does not occur, the therapist will burn out.

65

Interpersonal cohesiveness is one of the most powerful phenomena we can use as an indicator of excellence in therapy and to show that a therapist is on the right path to the existential in treatment. Yet this concept is the same for the beginnings of any relationship, and it can even help the "damaged" relationship. For example, if parents could strive to achieve a cohesive level of communication with their adolescents, an overall decrease in family conflict would occur.

In short, cohesiveness focuses on the relationship. Considering therapy, this relationship of cohesiveness concerns itself with the dynamics between the therapist and the participant in therapy. However, this scope can be broadened to include married couples, family members, and business peers. The principles found within the ideas of CORE can be utilized in several different arenas.

Many techniques can aid achieving cohesiveness. Within and without the psychotherapeutic sphere, the ideas of reflective listening, curious questions, open-ended questions, understanding others before expounding on your point of view, summarizing, affirming, and soul talk, as explained previously, can all lead to cohesiveness in any relationship. However, cohesiveness is more than just mere techniques; there must be emotional and spiritual components present before cohesion can occur. No algorithm on earth will lead to a truly cohesive relationship. The closest a person can get to an recipe for how to achieve cohesiveness is to follow the signposts along the way, such as using reflective listening, in combination with trusting his own heart.

Again, let me iterate, when considering all of these techniques, keep in mind that these are only tools to establishing a relationship. With many of the techniques, one last idea must be explored before cohesion can occur: you must realize, *it is not what you do with the other individual or group, but who you are.* If your heart is not in the communication—or you are distracted or apathetic, for example—cohesion will not be present in the relationship. Cohesion cannot be faked.

Remember, cohesion needs to be established before an exploration of insight, observations, or perspective transformation can begin. If cohesion has not been established in the relationship, a dispute or disagreement will occur.

In most of psychotherapeutic literature, the concept of resistance is the idea that the client or patient is opposing therapeutic change. Moreover, many therapists see resistance as an attitude for which the patient is solely responsible. I have heard terms such as *denial, projection, reaction*, and so on, used often when therapists have discussed "resistance." Of course, projection, denial, and other defenses do occur within an individual; however, resistance, I have found, occurs within the relationship between interviewer and participant. For this reason I am more comfortable using the terms *dispute* or *disagreement* when describing resistance in a therapy session. Indeed, the interviewer is just as responsible for a disagreement or dispute as the participant is. Thus, a disagreement should be used by an interviewer as a gauge that indicates that the relationship has become tangential. As a therapist, I attempt to remember that my goal is to help alleviate the four D's of destructiveness: distress, dysfunction, danger, and disturbance. Why are some therapists, parents, and spouses so eager to confront people when this confrontation will inevitably lead to the very behavior that the therapist, parent, or spouse wants to change, not to mention the fact that it will lead the participant, client, child, or spouse to a higher level of distress?

In the past, confrontation was often used in therapy, especially in the field of drug and alcohol treatment; however, recently it has been shown that confrontation only leads to an increase in disagreements and disputes within the therapeutic relationship. William Miller and Stephen Rollnick, in their book *Motivational Interviewing*, have given empirical evidence of the effectiveness of a more goal-oriented, person-centered approach to "preparing people for change." Considering the phenomenon of disagreements (resistance), Miller and Rollnick describe ways to "roll with it," thus supporting the "Spirit of Motivational Interviewing": being *collaborative, evocative*, and respecting an individual's *autonomy*. Miller and Rollnick agree that disagreements (resistance) in therapy occur within the relationship between interviewer and participant. They state, "We emphasize that, to a significant extent, resistance arises from the interpersonal interaction between counselor and client." They also add, "If resistance is increasing during counseling, it is very likely in response to something you (the counselor) are doing."[1]

Miller and Rollnick go on to describe ways to respond to disagreements when they arise. These include "reflective responses," such as "simple reflections (respond to resistance with nonresistance)," "amplified reflections (reflect back statements in an exaggerated form)," "double-sided reflections ('on the one hand you feel X; however, on the other side you feel Y')." Other responses to resistance are a little more strategic, yet hold to the principles of Motivational Interviewing. These include "Shifting Focus (shifting the participant's focus off the roadblock)," "Reframing (recasting the participant's information into a new meaning)," "Agreeing with a Twist (a reflection followed by a reframe)," "Emphasizing Personal Choice and Control," "Coming Alongside (getting the participant to fight for his/her own change)."[2] Remember, what we resist persists.

Motivational Interviewing contains powerful ideas in establishing cohesiveness between the interviewer and the participant in therapy. This is because of its focus on the intrinsic integrity of the individual and its authoritative style of "take what will help you and leave the rest."

Once the interviewer and participant are successful in establishing cohesion and agree that it is time to take action—indicated by the participant's readiness, willingness, and ability—Observation will arise.

Cohesive Activity:

Think of someone with whom you relationally struggle. How have you approached this person in the past? Were there things that you wanted to say but fear kept you from saying them? In an assertive stance, approach that person and tell him about yourself. Include items such as the things you enjoy doing and the goals you aspire to.

Attempt to achieve "soul talk." With a person with whom you have a close relationship, attempt to have a conversation full of themes concerning hopes, dreams, and desires to see if you are able to achieve soul talk as had been explained in the previous discussion.

NOTES

1. William R. Miller and Stephen Rollnick, *Motivational Interviewing: Preparing People for Change*, 2d ed. (New York: Guilford Press, 2002), 53–83.

2. Ibid.

Discussion 9

OBSERVATION

For now we see through a glass darkly; but then face to face: now I know in part; but then shall I know even as also I am known.
—1 Corinthians 13:12

THROUGH AN AWARENESS OF THE PAST and how past vulnerabilities have been psychologically influential, an individual can come to an acceptance of the past and in turn overcome it by choosing to do so. Acknowledging the hurt and looking at its effects will open a person up to his potential strengths. He must begin by looking at the effects from many different perspectives; this is why therapy is so crucial—you get a relatively unbiased viewpoint from a therapist, as opposed to the viewpoint of family members or friends.

As a person explores his or her past and the damage caused, he can easily get caught up in the blame game. This can be very tempting because it is easy to assign blame to an external object, but this can easily lead to victimhood. Playing the victim is very addictive because it gives a person a false sense of power. If you have the perspective of the victim, you feel as though you are not responsible and that people also notice you. And "blame" is all part of the game. If you are a victim, people feel sorry for you; you can be offended easily and take almost anything personally. A victim's reality is skewed significantly because he is essentially living a lie. In reality, every individual is a capable person who has much to offer the world, but a victim has undermined himself and created a big hole in his soul. As will be discussed later, to fully heal from trauma or pain, individuals must reframe the perspective of their "damaged lives" to ones of growth, thus becoming survivors and not victims (see Discussion 1). A big

69

difference exists between the two frames of mind. Survivors are responsible for themselves and their reality. Victims are only reactive, placing blame on outside forces for their pain (Externalization). An individual must not be tempted by the pull of pain. Focusing on a person's strengths helps that person to reframe his history.

One last note for therapists in particular: I have learned through years of conducting therapy that I can't use my client's session to rescue my own wounded child. I have found that this can happen with therapists, especially when it comes to cases of child abuse. Of course, in these cases of abuse, a report must be made; however, as therapists we must stay as objective as possible and not, as William Miller stated, "let the righting reflex"[1] destroy our therapeutic alliance with our clients.

Observation Activity

Write down the names of three people in your life who influenced your shadow self, people who were a source of shame for you.

Write down the names of three people who influenced the light self, in which they promoted authenticity and self-fulfillment.

This activity is a good exercise to aid in understanding why we do the things we do, because we are accepting sources of shame, the "A" in "REAL SELF."

NOTE

1. Miller and Rollnick, *Motivational Interviewing*, 53–83.

Discussion 10

RESILIENCY

And if your eye be single to my glory, your whole bodies shall be filled with light, and there shall be no darkness in you; and that body which is filled with light comprehendeth all things.

—Doctrine and Covenants 88:67

MANY RESEARCHERS, DEVELOPMENTALISTS, AND CLINICIANS CONJECTURE that there are essential core traits of resiliency. These could include creativity, initiative, having personal values, insight, a need to achieve, interdependence, and so on. To fully define all of the traits that encompass resiliency is beyond the scope of this exercise. I want to merely focus on the basic definition of resiliency and how the concept can help your own life situation and those whom you aid. One definition for resiliency is given by Steve and Sybil Wolin in their book *The Resilient Self.* They define resiliency as "your capacity to bounce back, to withstand hardship and repair yourself."[1]

One aspect of resiliency includes an awareness or focus on a positive perspective, or optimism. For example, resiliency is the difference between those who see themselves as victims of a traumatic event and those who see themselves as survivors, as explained in our discussion on observation. To continue with this example, imagine ten people were attacked by a violent person. Five considered themselves victims and five survivors. The difference between these people is that the former would be haunted by the event and would focus their mental energies on notions of revenge and self-pity, while the latter would transcend the event by accepting the fact that there are "bad people" in the world and they, the survivors, have the choice not to be affected by those events and people. Many resilient individuals turn adversity into advantage, they term problems as "challenges," and they are proactive and responsible in determining the outcomes of their lives.

I once met a man who as a boy ran away from a dysfunctional home where he was physically and emotionally abused. At the age of twelve, he found himself on the street, with no money, no shelter, and no resources. He said of the night that he ran away, "I was so frightened, but I had to leave. My family was taking more away from me than I would lose by living homeless." The first week was extremely difficult. Scared, cold, and physically exhausted, he met a nineteen-year-old homeless man who introduced him to his friends. This group of young men formed a sort of coalition: they would look out for each other. During the day, one boy would beg in front of a business, while another would work odd jobs. Another boy would gather broken crates to burn for heat that night, while another would gather any object available to use for shelter. These boys did not complain about their predicament; they were too focused on solving immediate problems and resolving needs. Eventually, after two years on the street, the police picked up the once twelve-year-old runaway, and child protective services placed him with a distant relative. Reflecting on this experience, the gentleman stated, "I learned more about life and strategies to overcome pain and challenges during that time period than any other experience I had gained ten years after the fact."

What needs to be in place to enable a person to become resilient? First, an essential ingredient is a belief in your intrinsic ability to influence your personal life. Second, self-efficacy in knowing that your intrinsic ability can influence your environment. After these beliefs are established, resiliency exponentially increases as an individual achieves success in life and has the evidence of his own competence.

Observation Activity

The seven resiliency traits described by Wolin and Wolin are independence, insight, relationships, humor, creativity, initiative, and morality. Identify which trait is currently your strongest and why. Then identify which two traits are your weakest and why. Establish two goals you want to do to increase your resiliency in these areas. For example: "I feel relationships are my weakness, because I like to do things on my own, I live alone and work alone. I would like to reach out to others more by joining a book group."

NOTE

1. Steve and Sybil Wolin, *The Resilient Self: How Survivors of Troubled Families Rise above Adversity* (New York: Villard Books, 1993).

Discussion 11

EXISTENTIAL

To live is to suffer, to survive is to find meaning in the suffering.
—Victor Frankl

THE EXISTENTIAL HAS BEEN MUCH REITERATED throughout this text. However, it would be advantageous to revisit some key aspects of this idea.

Answers to the "terrible questions" are found through the study of existentialism and in the understanding of the transpersonal and spiritual. Life is fraught with peril and pain, and the most effective way to overcome suffering is to understand the meaning behind it. The existential should always be addressed before ending a therapeutic relationship because without this understanding, any behavioral modifications, shifts in perspective, or anything else in therapy loses its effectiveness. For example, how can an individual be expected to overcome a crippling addiction by merely staying away from outside forces that encourage triggers without changing his spiritual focus and relying on a higher power?

For life in general, an understanding of the existential can lead to a fulfilling experience of personal efficacy, or an understanding that you have control over yourself and that you can influence your environment. The *first and last freedom* for any individual is to realize that he has a choice. Many mental disorders and existential crises cannot overcome the idea that a person has agency in the matter. Ultimately, we are all free to feel the way that we do. Assuming full responsibility for the cause of our mood or behavior is liberating. This is something that I attempt to instill in all those with whom I work before they finish a therapeutic encounter;

once this is realized, these people no longer need me—and in my opinion, that is successful therapy. A profound statement was made by one of my clients: "We are responsible for everything . . . ourselves, our neighbor, the starving children in Africa . . . but we are not to blame." That kind of insight can lead to freedom and joy.

It is crucial that the existential becomes the focus of therapy before the therapeutic relationship ends. And the seeds of spirituality should be continuously addressed throughout therapy, even beginning with the first session. Again, the reasoning for this is that ultimate healing can only occur through an understanding of ultimate meaning and as the individual's soul (heart, body, and spirit) are united toward an ultimate goal.

People usually know when the encounter between therapist-participant, mother-child, friend-friend, or spouse-spouse has shifted to the existential, for the conversation will have undertoned themes of spiritual talk, the meaning of life, relationships, God, and so on. One question I have used to spark an existential conversation is, "What do you think is the purpose of all of this?" For example, once when discussing a young man's experiences with exorbitant loss, I asked, "Why do you think all of this happened to you . . . what is the meaning behind all of this loss you have suffered?" Again, in any interpersonal encounter, the relationship is solidified once the spiritual side of each individual in the relationship is processed, whether this is in a romantic, parental, platonic, or therapeutic relationship.

As stated in this text, existentialism focuses on responsibility, which is the antithesis of denying responsibility on the basis of psychodynamic forces or of "psychic determinism." Existentialism also discusses the balance between extremes in every individual. The notion of individual uniqueness leads to the idea of every person being mutually exclusive of others, and thus one cannot realistically be diagnosed. This concept is analogous to every fingerprint having its own pattern. Every individual is an individual, and no one else is like that individual.

Existential Activity:

Write down as many personal fears and anxieties as you are aware of, and then write down why these are your fears and anxieties. Complete the activity by discussing your faith and your strengths and how these aspects of yourself diminish your fears and anxieties.

Process:
EXAMPLE CASE OF
CORE

WHILE PROGRESSING THROUGH A THERAPEUTIC ENCOUNTER or session with the participant, one must focus on the four quadrants of CORE: Cohesiveness, Observation (curious questions, restatements, reframes), a focus on the Resiliency, and finally, guidance toward the Existential.

Since CORE transformation aligns itself with a person-centered, transpersonal approach, I hesitate to give a case example. Indeed, the majority of CORE interviews need to be spontaneous, with minimal formal preparation; thus, authenticity can occur in the interviewer-participant relationship. Moreover, there are limits to the amount of information and experience gained from one observation of a clinical case. No one example can include all of the richness and diversity gained through participation in a variety of therapy encounters, especially the example is through writing. However, our discussion necessitates a detailed example of the CORE approach in order to gain an understanding of the *what* and the *how* of utilizing this philosophy. Of course, many things will be missing from this experience because of the limitations of a two-dimensional written account of the interview. For example, the interviewer and the participant in the following example became deeply involved in the mutual dialogue which took place—essentially they both began to soul talk with one another, as described in the previous discussion on cohesion. Of course, this cannot be experienced by reading the account, or even watching the account. One must participate in order to soul talk.

The encounter to be presented is that of a twenty-nine-year-old business executive who came for consultation so she could gain an understanding of her mixed anxiety and depression. She also had a severe drinking problem, which she had expressed on an intake questionnaire as "not a big deal." However, her spouse had stated on his intake questionnaire that her drinking had caused her to miss days at work, and her associates had indicated to him that they were concerned. She'd had previous therapy sessions and indicated that they had not helped. Her previous therapist had stated that she was "difficult and resistive" and indicated that the participant wouldn't finish the therapeutic assignments. According to her previous therapist, this woman "merely wanted to be in therapy to complain about how horrible her life was." The participant went to therapy after a discussion with her husband helped her realize that she was depressed and anxious and that she had been for quite some time.

The following encounter will be an example of the use of CORE as the session evolves:

INTERVIEWER: Hello. Please have a seat, wherever you like. We can take about fifty minutes today, and the time is yours. What would you like to discuss?

Emphasizing choice. Evaluating her level of self-efficacy. Minor boundary setting. Utilization of open question to promote Cohesion between interviewer and participant.

PARTICIPANT: Oh, I was talking to my husband the other day about why I have been feeling so worn out lately. I started to realize that I couldn't remember when I didn't feel worn out. After talking about my physical exhaustion, my husband asked, "Do you think you might be depressed?" I actually got offended at first, but then I started thinking, "You know, I do feel like I have a big pit in the middle of me." I don't know . . . I mean, I feel sad sometimes, but I also can't keep my mind off things, you know?

Participant begins to set up the Observation—She vocalizes initial awareness of underlying problems; essentially she sees the branches but is unaware of the root.

INTERVIEWER: So you have been feeling physically exhausted and your husband stated that you might be depressed. After saying this to you, you began to think about the feeling of having a "big pit" in the middle of you. You also can't get your mind off things. What things can't you keep your mind off?

Interviewer restates to continue to establish Cohesion and reinforce Observation/ Awareness made by participant.

PARTICIPANT: Well, a lot of times, I worry about things at work, when I am at home . . . I mean, it is like I worry that the business is going to fall apart if I am not there. I don't know. Maybe it is irrational but I think things will just fall apart if I'm not monitoring everything, you know?

INTERVIEWER: If you are not in control, things can turn to chaos.

Amplification to assess participant's level of anxiety.

PARTICIPANT: Well, kinda. Not really chaos, but I think to myself "Bad things could happen at work if I am not there," you know?

INTERVIEWER: What bad things?

PARTICIPANT: I don't know . . . a customer could be calling because his account is a mess, or one of the employees could have misfiled things . . . or . . . you know.

INTERVIEWER: And these things would have to be taken care of immediately. If an employee misfiled something, it would have to be taken care of ASAP.

PARTICIPANT: Well, no. It just . . . it just is so hard sometimes.

Participant becomes tearful.

INTERVIEWER: Things can be difficult.

Almost thirty seconds of silence elapses.

PARTICIPANT: I don't know. Life . . . I mean, there are so many things to worry about—the mortgage, the business, my family, my husband's job. You know, his company might be downsizing (pause), and he might be out of a job (pause).

INTERVIEWER: (pause)

PARTICIPANT: I would just hate to be the one who brings home all of the bacon. He (husband) is such a "man," and I think that will be hard for him to not have a job . . . I don't know. Sometimes I just want to (pause).

INTERVIEWER: Want to . . . ?

PARTICIPANT: Sometimes I just want to run away, get away from it all. Go to a desert island and be alone.

INTERVIEWER: Have you ever just escaped? Have you ever just left it all?

PARTICIPANT: Well, no . . . what do you mean?

Participant is gaining insight/observation

INTERVIEWER: Have you ever run away from a problem that you felt you couldn't handle?

PARTICIPANT: Yeah, I guess. When I was sixteen my parents would fight a lot. I mean, they would swear at each other and call each other names. One day—I must have been a junior in high school—they started fighting and I went up to my dad and said, "If you guys don't shut up, I'm leaving." (laughing) I mean his face became so red, he couldn't say anything! But I knew I was dead. I ran out of the house as fast as I could and went to a friend's house. I stayed there overnight, and then I spent another week at my aunt's house. I did *not* want to face my dad (pause).

INTERVIEWER: I'm curious. What was going through your mind and how were you feeling during that time away from home? And have you ever felt the same way any time recently?

Curious question to establish and reinforce observation.

PARTICIPANT: Well, when I ran away from home, I remember being angry and scared. Um . . . I was mad at my parents . . . I mean, why couldn't they just get along? You know, they still fight to this day.

INTERVIEWER: So even now, your parents battle it out.

PARTICIPANT: Yeah, I mean, they are both almost sixty. I don't know why they just don't get a divorce! But anyway, I did feel mad when I ran away in high school. What was your other question?

INTERVIEWER: Have you felt the same way lately?

PARTICIPANT: Sure I have. I get angry and I get scared (pause, and silence for about 10 seconds). Like I said, things can just get so difficult!

INTERVIEWER: Difficult things can make you angry and scared.

PARTICIPANT: You know, work of course is difficult. I work with a lot of people who don't know what they are doing. My husband can get me frustrated. I don't know . . . a lot of things.

INTERVIEWER: Work and your relationship with your husband can be difficult as well.

PARTICIPANT: Yeah. And the future. What is going to happen to my husband's job? Things like that.

INTERVIEWER: You know, some people say that anger usually stems from pain, guilt or fear. You said that you had run away from home because of fear toward your dad and the pain that their fights were causing you. Is that correct?

PARTICIPANT: Yes.

INTERVIEWER: How do you run away from the pain and the fear today?

PARTICIPANT: I don't know. Sometimes I think I block it out.

INTERVIEWER: Block it out? What do you mean by block it out?

PARTICIPANT: I will try to flood myself with work. So I don't think too much. Thinking too much can lead to pain, because I will think of the wrong things. You know, my mind can just go a mile an hour!

INTERVIEWER: So you block it out by working, because thinking too much can lead to pain. You used the word *flood*. What do you mean by "flood"?

PARTICIPANT: I guess I mean that I try to work as much as possible.

INTERVIEWER: You also said that you flood yourself with work to keep yourself from thinking, because you will think of the wrong things. What are the wrong things?

PARTICIPANT: I don't know.

(long pause)

PARTICIPANT: I don't know (becomes tearful). I think of hurting myself when I get stressed.

INTERVIEWER: There has been a lot of pain in your life, and it sounds like the stress can be unbearable.

PARTICIPANT: Yeah. (pause)

INTERVIEWER: Have you ever hurt yourself in the past?

PARTICIPANT: Yes. I have cut myself, and I have used drugs.

INTERVIEWER: Have you ever been suicidal?

PARTICIPANT: Of course, but I just have random thoughts about it. I would never actually do it.

INTERVIEWER: You never really had a plan, but you have had thoughts about it.

At this point in the interview, the interviewer has focused on establishing cohesiveness, observation, and personal insight. The interviewer has also begun to assess suicidal tendencies after the participant reported self-harm.

This assessment definitely has a different feel than a mutual dialogue. The interviewer became more of an inquisitor than an interviewer; however, this had to happen because the participant vocalized personal harm. The interviewer will return to the cohesion and observation, since the participant reported no plan or intent to carry out suicide.

It is interesting to note that most of the interviewer's responses up to this point have been in the form of curious open questions. At a few points thus far, the interviewer made some affirmations, such as expressing empathy for the pain that the participant has lived through. Also the interviewer used summarizations to aid the cohesive process. More than mere reflections, summarizations let those with whom you are in dialogue know that you are really attempting to understand their point of view.

At this point the interviewer is also assessing the participant's willingness to discuss her substance abuse. Since she volunteered the information that she has used drugs in the past, this is an indicator that a certain level of cohesion has been established to proceed to the observation of her past alcohol usage. If the participant had not volunteered this information, the interviewer would have continued to establish more cohesion with this participant. The reasoning for this is that if a certain level of cohesiveness has not been established, the participant's willingness to discuss hurtful topics will be met with stalemates between the interviewer and the participant. Remember, resistance in any relationship occurs between two people; it would not totally be the participant's fault if she did not want to discuss her substance use after the interviewer pushed it.

INTERVIEWER: You said that you have used drugs. May I ask you what drugs?

PARTICIPANT: Yes. Well, I admit, lately I have been drinking a little. I have used marijuana some years ago, but only a few times. In high school, me and some friends used to do "whip-its" at parties. . . . Oh yeah, and some of my friends and I would crush up the candy Smarties and sniff it in middle school. But I guess that really isn't a drug. (laugh/pause) I think that is about it.

INTERVIEWER: So recently, you have been drinking a little, but really nothing else for some years.

PARTICIPANT: Yeah.

INTERVIEWER: As we have been sitting here today, I have been impressed by how open you are with me; you seem like a strong individual. What are some of your strengths? What do you do well?

PARTICIPANT: Well, I like to golf, is that what you mean?

INTERVIEWER: Well, perhaps, but I am looking for character strengths. I want to know what helps you get through difficult times, or even what gives you purpose and meaning in your life?

PARTICIPANT: Um, that is kinda difficult. I don't know. Well, I don't know if I think about it much. I guess I am a hard worker. My job gives me a lot of self-esteem. I also look forward to my job.

INTERVIEWER: Your job gives you purpose.

PARTICIPANT: Sure. Maybe I am a workaholic. I mean, I actually enjoy being at work more than other places—well, except Hawaii (laugh).

(pause)

PARTICIPANT: Um, I used to have a lot of hobbies. I would scrapbook, go golfing, read.

The interviewer decided to refocus his attention on the participant's strengths, because the participant was making it clear through her metacommunication that she was becoming anxious about his questions concerning her drinking. The interviewer changed focus to decrease any roadblocks that the participant might have placed if this line of questioning had continued.

It is interesting to note that the interviewer went directly from inquiring about her substance abuse to having her describe her strengths. This is very useful to do when a participant becomes too negative, especially if the participant begins to play the archetypical martyr or victim. Refocusing on strengths can greatly increase an individual's sense of resiliency, capability, and efficacy.

INTERVIEWER: Read—what do you like to read?

PARTICIPANT: Books that have substance. Books that I can sink my teeth into and will move me.

INTERVIEWER: Books that are in-depth.

PARTICIPANT: Yes. I love to just lose myself in a book . . . You know, when you are so into the book that you are not even aware of your surroundings anymore . . . that is the kind of books I like.

INTERVIEWER: You enjoy the escape.

PARTICIPANT: Yeah, you know life can be so hard; it is nice to just escape.

INTERVIEWER: Is it difficult at times for you to lose yourself in a book, even though it is a good book? I mean, is life sometimes too difficult that a book isn't enough of a distraction?

PARTICIPANT: Yes. I think that is why I have used substances. I mean, you know, to escape.

Considering the above excerpt, it can be observed that the interviewer/therapist follows a philosophy of CORE, that is, the interviewer considers the idea that the participant should be doing most of the talking and work. If a therapist finds himself doing the majority of the exertion in therapy, then therapy may be helping the therapist more than it is helping the participant. It is essential to remember that through suffering and toil, growth and wisdom will develop.

The things that will save us:

POLITICS WITH PRINCIPLE;
PLEASURE WITH CONSCIENCE;
WEALTH WITH WORK;
KNOWLEDGE WITH CHARACTER;
BUSINESS WITH MORALITY;
SCIENCE WITH HUMANITY;
WORSHIP WITH SACRIFICE.

PHILOSOPHY & VISION

As we can see, almost every mental health issue is either indirectly or directly influenced by a lack of love.

—Anonymous

Note: *Originally, this appendix was the introduction of this book. I realized that many of these concepts discussed in this section described a philosophical background, thus making it a confusing introduction. A new introduction was subsequently written. Aspects of this section read as though it were the introduction.*

IN WRITING *HEALING SECRETS: Self-Medicating Our Most Important Relationships*, I came to a realization that as with any person who bestows information or gives advice, I was essentially writing to myself—or basically giving myself ideas on how to increase my love for others and overcome my own narcissistic ego (self-centeredness) and biased ways. And indeed, when I discuss concepts such as the camp of the universalist, or the personality state of transcendence, I am fully aware that I do not inhabit these states even five percent of the time—although I do have the vision and desire to attain and maintain these states. I know that I must increasingly practice discipline and self-sacrifice to progress toward these goals.

It is an interesting life that each one of us lives, and it is fascinating to consider the mode and momentum each one of us develops in maturity and intelligence. For some this development is rapid, with both emotion and intellect developing in tandem; for others, development of either intellect or emotion is fixated at a particular moment in time. This is especially true for those who have experienced and repressed trauma. As for myself, my development was sporadic, but I found that the times in which I had the greatest spikes in my personal development were those times in which I focused on my spiritual self, or when I trusted in the will of God. This trust in God led me to an understanding of acceptance . . . acceptance of pain, suffering, sorrows, the meaningless nature of the world, and life itself. Much like the individual in a twelve-step program who, in essence, realizes that his sobriety can only be accomplished by his reliance on a higher power, I have come to the awareness that all pain, depression, anxiety, neuroticism, and psychosis can be totally healed only determination spiritual effort. With a focus on "the big questions"—or even on those inquiries that Hugh Nibley refers to as "the terrible questions"—a person receives a broader perspective of his life. If an individual can come close to conceptualizing his eternal future, many of the day-to-day doldrums do not seem as significant.

Healing Secrets as a philosophy is devoted to the perspective of existentialism. As a psychology, these ideas are married to concepts found in transpersonalism (psychology focused on an individual's spiritual nature). And as psychotherapy, the book is aligned with the person-centered approach (therapy focused on choice and autonomy), especially when considering the ideas of CORE, which stands for Cohesiveness, Observation (awareness/insight), Resiliency, and Existentialism. And indeed, as with any similar document, most of my awareness comes from my belief system, first and foremost as a deeply committed spiritual individual and second as an ever-progressing psychotherapist. Again, with all of these things considered, the reasoning for the devotion to the existential, transpersonal, and person-centeredness in this document are these:

Insight: The key to any attitudinal, emotional, or behavioral shift is to focus on the idea that these traits do not necessarily change; rather, they develop, or evolve, similar to maturity development, which occurs along a continuum of growth. Basically, all that psychotherapy can accomplish is a reframe or a shift in an individual's perspective—and indeed, only if the client chooses this. Certainly, psychotherapy reframes perception, if it is skewed, distorted, or utterly delusional. But when a therapist attempts to take on the challenge of changing another, that therapist will become frustrated and eventually burn out, because a therapist can't change anyone—all he can do is attempt to be a guide as a person develops. And the way to do this as a therapist is to first understand the person who is seeking help by validating, actively listening, affirming, restating, and so on, and then helping individuals reframe their perception by being curious, and noticing patterns and discrepancies, and bringing an awareness of these patterns to the individual in a non-judgmental, evocative, and actively engaging fashion.

Meaning: Existentialism and transpersonalism are heavily imbued in ideas concerning ultimate meaning, such as "Why are we here on earth?" and "What is our purpose?" These "terrible questions" are seen as the foundation of healing. And when the spiritual foundations—principles, values, virtues—of an individual are focused upon or repaired, his behaviors, attitudes, emotions, and thoughts will follow.

Members of the helping professions have long addressed the issues surrounding existential angst in the form of alienation as it manifests itself in disorders of mood and behavior. Existential person-centered therapy and existential analysis have considered the alienating problems of dread, isolation, despair, boredom, doubt, guilt, anger, and fear or anxiety. Historically, existential therapy and analysis was introduced around the World War II era, with such contributors as Victor Frankl and his ideas of logotherapy, and with the works of Rollo May.

Recently, however, the existential modes of therapy have been overshadowed by "quick fix" techniques such as cognitive therapy and rational emotive behavioral therapy (specifically in North America), which can be very effective models of therapy. However, these forms of treatment can actually contribute to alienation if they are not followed up by a more spiritually oriented therapy. The "quick fix" therapies do this by emphasizing a distorted notion that suffering is pointless and that one should minimize pain and replace it with a type of hedonistic happiness. Discussing existentialism, Gordon Allport stated, "The central theme of existentialism: to live is to suffer, to survive is to find meaning in the suffering."[1] More so than ever, our society is isolating itself. Active involvement and concern for other human beings are being drowned out by the noise of commercialism. The existential problems of disconnectedness to others, dread, anger, and self-preoccupation are exponentially increasing. As a society, we need to connect once again with each other—this is what makes us human, and this is what inspires.

Agency: Choice is the key. Forcefulness and coercion have no place in an existential/transpersonal person-centered approach. Furthermore, the concepts and notions of psychic determinism, which Freudian psychoanalysis espouses, are the antithesis to choice and free will, *minima non curat praetor*. Basically, Sigmund Freud stated: "But so far as I can observe, it [free will] does not manifest itself in weighty and important decisions; on these occasions, one has much more the feeling of a psychic compulsion and gladly falls back upon it . . . What is thus left free from the one side receives its motives from the other side, from the unconscious, and the determinism in the psychic realm is thus carried out uninterruptedly."[2]

In some other forms, Freudianism hints of a type of circular causation, free-will—determinism—free will—determinism; however, the outcome in this theory always concludes with a type of total psychic determinism. Freud again discusses, "Many persons argue against the assumption of an absolute psychic determinism by referring to an intense feeling of conviction that there is a free will. This feeling exists, but is not incompatible with the belief in determinism."[3]

Though it certainly has its shortcomings, this mode of psychotherapy can be very beneficial to individuals, especially people who suffer from attachment issues. Therapies and theories, such as object relation, ego psychology, psychosociality, and so on, are valid and impactful modes of treatment, in this author's opinion.

On the other hand, the ideas of total psychic determinism can be negatively enabling and disempowering. Determinism suspends a sense of personal and social responsibility and gives way to the excuses like, "this is the way I am," "this is what I was born to be," and "I will never change or grow." Instead of seeing psychosocial stresses as only influences, those who are *determined* by these stressors live a life of relinquishing responsibility, which in turn disables their personal growth. Many who have been addicted to substances use determinism as an excuse: "I come from a long line of alcoholics—it is in the blood . . . I guess this is what I will turn out to be . . . an alcoholic."

Not only do Freudian psychiatrists ascribe to the ideas of determinism, there are other ideas that go beyond the notion of psychic determinism. There are anthropological ideas of genetic determinism, such as "it is in the gene pool." Notions of social and environmental determinism can be found in theories of sociology and social work; for example, there is a belief that the socioeconomic class that a person is born into determines his future status in society will be.

Essentially, the theory of determinism is a smoke screen, a justification to legitimize certain social sciences; it undermines basic principles and gives idleness an excuse. However, the concepts of free will and choice are empowering. When an individual realizes that he has control over his life, the individual overcomes ideas of "destiny" and changes his life to come into line with his goals and objectives. The serenity prayer of AA fame puts these notions of free will, choice, and control in a clear perspective:

> God grant me the serenity
> To accept the things I cannot change,
> The courage to change the things I can,
> And the wisdom to know the difference.[4]

Integrity: As a society, values, principles, and morals are losing meaning. Have you ever played a game in which all participants decided to change the rules to the point where everyone was cheating? Admittedly, I did this as a youth, and I noticed that after only a few minutes, the game became pointless. On a grander scale, our society is doing the same thing—cheating! And with principles disappearing, so are purpose and meaning. Humankind is losing its symbols and myths, and this is leading to a diminished depth of our hearts. Existential and transpersonalism focuses on bigger ideas and truths, which transcend superficialities in which people so easily get entangled.

As mentioned above, choice is essential, free will must happen to heal, and considering the ideas of core principles, moral agency must be considered as a foundation for a person to truly overcome weaknesses and limitations. Moral agency refers to the decision of right and wrong where freedom and ethics intersect. The ideas of personal character are being lost in our increasingly narcissistic society. Indeed, as society focuses only on the accumulation of things (a narcissistic perspective), the purposes of humanity and life become superseded in perception by those who pledge themselves to this lifestyle. Truly, when spiritual dissonance (or an incongruence of behavior and values) occurs, personal values are suspended. Depression and angst will soon follow. This idea of spiritual dissonance is plaguing society; it explains the increased cases of mood disorders, character disorders, substance abuse, and other addictions.

In substance abuse specifically, once a person experiences the existential incongruence between his actions or attitudes and his deep core principles (as long as those actions are maintained), the pain caused by such incongruence is drowned out by the mind-numbing effect of illicit substances. With all of this said, there must be emphasis placed on the existential to restore harmony between surface attitudes and behaviors and the spiritual nature of the human.

Personal Responsibility: Existential and transpersonalism focuses on meaning. Nietzsche stated, "He who has a why to live can bear with almost any how." This means if an individual has a purpose, a vision, or a reason, that person can deal with any issue, pain, or roadblock that stands in the way of that vision. Essentially, with consideration and focus on the spiritual, a person can choose to have an attitude change and perceive life in a different light. Many traditional psychotherapies nowadays focus on the management of symptoms (behavioral modification, medication management, behavioral management, thought journaling) but neglect the core reason for that management being in place. This might explain the high recidivism in many behavioral-modifying treatment centers. Indeed, in many of these centers, the focus is placed on achieving short-term goals on a treatment plan, with the ultimate objective being placed on finishing the program. If vision is this limited, the individual participating in treatment is substantially weakened. Existentialism places meaning and vision at the forefront of therapy. Focusing on reason and meaning is much more of a motivating factor for most people than centering focus on contingencies.

One aspect of psychotherapy I have observed is the cold and calculating tendencies that many therapies can exhibit, and these characteristics are perceived as such by those individuals being treated. Diagnostic labels are used so often that they become the diagnosis. Diagnostics has a deterministic flavor to it. For example, I have heard someone once say, "I am bipolar; that is why I can't hold down a job." This individual said this as easily as most of us would say, "Hi, my name is Jim, and I like to golf." Essentially, this person who had bipolar issues was implicitly saying, "I am my label, and I am disabled, so don't ask me to do anything and don't rely on me." And so responsibility avoidance set in. And indeed, this motivation was discovered after a few sessions of therapy.

Moreover, the cold and calculating tendencies of many psychotherapies can further be explained by the overall self-absorbed ideals of society
in general. Essentially, the therapist simply "buys" into the culture and
the culture is unhealthy. The narcissist's need is fulfilled as the ego is
stroked, the quick-fix strategies bolster the narcissistic ego, giving the false
sense of "think happy, be happy." I have also wondered whether therapists are sometimes involved with psychotherapy for narcissistic reasons.
A practitioner may ask himself, "Do I treat people because I enjoy the role
of healthy healer over the sick or disabled?" If the answer is "yes," therapy
is motivated by vanity—promoting the ego by surrounding oneself with
"lessers." This can also be called a top-down approach to therapy. The
practitioner who attempts to keep the "therapist face" on at the expense of
authenticity undermines the therapeutic relationship.

As a therapist, I have learned that to fully understand humankind, I
must explore the intricacies of literature, art, and religion. For me, therapy
is as much an art as it is a science, and perhaps psychotherapy may even be
more of an art! Spontaneity is found in psychotherapy, as truly it is within
art. Behavioral science performs excellently when it concerns itself with
the description of surface behaviors and observable phenomena, but only
through the understanding of the immeasurable conception of the heart
and the soul—through meaning and spirituality—can the lasting effects
of a therapeutic approach come into fruition.

As therapy progresses, I have found that the discussions become ever
increasingly motivated by spirituality. When a participant has an "a-ha"
moment, I have felt the inspiration and the Spirit in the room. Behavioral,
cognitive, emotional, and attitudinal changes are all just surface layers of
the spiritual core of the person. As the participant realizes his potential
and comes into awareness of his personal meaning, real change is present,
and a shifting point is achieved to set a precedent for the rest of his life.

I have found that the etiologies of pain are numerous. The reasons for
uncovering a person's potentials are abundant. This world is cruel, and it
treats its children cruelly. As a society, families are falling apart, and the
pain and suffering will continue exponentially as the cruelty is passed on
from one generation to another. Interventions need to occur. The more
people can involve themselves with helping others, especially children, the
more resilient people can become. And resiliency will lead to strength to
overcome damage caused by cruelty.

I am in search of meaning and purpose, and as I have stated previously, my motivation to write this document came about by gaining a desire to understand deep existential questions. Yet one thing that I have discovered as I have worked in my profession is that *almost every mental health issue is either indirectly or directly influenced by a lack of love.* And this book is my argument for this hypothesis.

NOTES

1. Gordon Allport, preface to *Man's Search for Meaning,* by Viktor Frankl (Boston: Beacon Press, 1992), 7.

2. Sigmund Freud, *Psychopathology of Everyday Life* (1938) in *The Basic Writings of Sigmund Freud,* trans. and ed. A. A. Brill (New York: Modern Library, 1995), 129–30.

3. Ibid.

4. Alcoholics Anonymous World Services, *Alcoholics Anonymous "The Big Book"* 3rd ed. 1976. From web based "blue book" (under "AA traditions"). See www.alcoholicsanonymous.com.

Appendix 2

THE JUNGIAN ARCHETYPE OVERVIEW

THE CONCEPT OF THE "LIGHT" vs. the "shadow" (Discussion 1) is associated with Jungian archetypes. An archetype is a psychological pattern taken from historical themes of life, such as the mother, child, trickster, prostitute, servant, death, or rebirth. The following is a list of common archetypes that function within most of us, with each item exhibiting a "light" side and a "shadow" side.

JUNGIAN ARCHETYPES

Actor	Healer	Provocateur
Addict	Hermit	Puppet
Alchemist	Historian	Puritan
Anarchist	Innovator	Rebel
Artist	Judge	Redeemer
Avenger	Knight	Rescuer
Beggar	Liberator	Revolutionary
Bully	Lover	Robot
Bureaucrat	Magical Child	Saboteur
Caregiver	Magician	Sadist
Child	Martyr	Sage
Clown	Masochist	Samaritan
Companion	Midas	Scholar
Coward	Monk	Scout
Crook	Muse	Scribe
Damsel	Mystic	Seductress
Detective	Nature	Seeker
Diva	Networker	Servant
Dictator	Nun	Settler
Dilettante	Olympian	Sidekick
Diplomat	Orphan Child	Slave
Disciple	Patriarch	Spoiler
Divine Child	Pilgrim	Storyteller
Dreamer	Pioneer	Student
Eternal Child	Poet	Teacher
Evangelist	Politician	Thief
Fool	Predator	Trickster
Gaia	Priest	Tyrant
Gambler	Prince	Victim
God	Princess	Visionary
Goddess	Prophet	Warrior
Gossip	Prostitute	

As we look at the preceding list, we can find archetypes that function within us. These archetypes influence our perception of life; however, we can choose how these influences dictate our behavior and attitude. Some archetypes have a greater hold on our attention. Take a look at the list and consider the archetypes that may be influencing you, then ask, "What does it mean that this archetype plays a powerful role in my life?" Remember, each of these has a "light" and "shadow" side. And keep in mind, what could be seen as a negative image, such as the prostitute, could function within us. Consider this: Do you ever give in to others' desires for you, or do you ever live up to another's agenda in violation of your own values? You may have the prostitute operational within you.

Essentially, within all of us there is a light side and a shadow side—the divine and the devilish, the toxic and the healthy, but we must not harshly judge either the light or shadow; we must merely identify, accept, and grow.

ABOUT THE AUTHOR

JADE MANGUS ATTENDED GRADUATE SCHOOL AT the University of Utah and has been a practicing counselor since 2004. He has written many professional articles directed toward the study of psychotherapy, specifically addiction treatment. He has made professional presentations through LDS Family Services, the University of Utah, and the Association of Mormon Counselors and Psychotherapists (AMCAP). He is currently president of AAIM Counseling in West Jordan, Utah.

Jade lives in West Jordan, Utah, with his wife, Jeralyne, and their two children, Sadie and Seth.